P9-DFJ-707

The Magic of Dogs

BOOKS BY BILL TARRANT

Best Way to Train Your Gun Dog

Bill Tarrant's Gun Dog Book: A Treasury of Happy Tails

Hey Pup, Fetch It Up! The Complete Retriever Training Book

Problem Gun Dogs

Tarrant Trains Gun Dogs

Training the Hunting Retriever: The New Approach

How to Hunt Birds with Gun Dogs

Pick of the Litter

The Magic of Dogs

The Magic of Dogs

Bill Tarrant

Lyons & Burford, Publishers

Copyright ©1995 by Bill Tarrant
ALL RIGHTS RESERVED. No part of this book may be reproduced in any manner without the express written consent of the publisher, except in the case of brief excerpts in critical reviews and articles.
All inquiries should be addressed to
Lyons & Burford, Publishers
31 West 21st Street, New York, NY 10010

Printed in the United States of America
Design by Kathy Kikkert
10 9 8 7 6 5 4 3 2 1

Library of Congress Cataloging-in-Publication Data
Tarrant, Bill.
The magic of dogs / Bill Tarrant.
p. cm.
ISBN 1-55821-365-1 (cloth)
1. Dog—Training. 2. Dogs—Behavior. 3. Human-animal relationships. 4. Dogs. I. Title.
SF431.T37 1995
636.7'0887—dc20 *95-21843*
CIP

Portions of chapter 16 first appeared in different form in Field & Stream, *July 1988. Portions of chapter 15 first appeared in different form in* Field & Stream, *March 1976. Portions of chapter 6 first appeared in different form in* Hey Pup, Fetch It Up! *Stackpole Books, 1979. Portions of chapter 3 first appeared in* Tarrant Trains Gun Dogs, *Stackpole Books, 1989.*

All photographs by Bill Tarrant unless otherwise noted.

For Muffy

Contents

PART ONE

THE MAGIC OF DOGS

1

The Magic of Dogs

The American Indians told their white-eyed conquerors, "God made the earth, and sun, and moon. He made man and bird and beast. But He didn't make the dog. He already had one."

Scholars who study philosophy or religion use the word *ineffable,* which means "that which is beyond explanation or description."

I find dogs ineffable. Magical, if you will. Mysterious and deep and phenomenal. It's because of this I brood so about man's inhumanity to life; man brutalizing a dog in the name of training. If we only knew how sensitive, and seventh-dimensioned, and totally unfathomable the dog is, we'd put away our heavy hands and loud voices forever. We'd bring along Pup so he'd reward us with the magic of a love-trained dog. And that's what we'll accomplish in this book.

Now, I'm not talking about Poopsy-woopsys, with fluffed hair-dos, painted nails, and fluorescent rain boots. I'm talking about you being a human being and Pup being a dog and the two of you giving each other the best you've got.

THE POINT OF VIEW

I've been a working-dog man for forty years and have written to the world about it for the last thirty. My specialty has been dogs who sniff bombs, herd sheep, fetch ducks, corner thieves in dark warehouses, dig hapless victims from avalanches, lead the blind, listen for the deaf, and become arms and legs for the paraplegic.

I've been the most impressed watching dogs make their rounds in a hospital, giving life back to the aged, diseased, and infirm who had—until that dog entered the ward—no more reason for living. And why do I appreciate these dogs most? *Because any dog can do it.* That's right. It's just the miraculous essence of the dog. To soothe, to heal, to rekindle the spirit and bring peace to the heart. Junkyard dog, alley dog, big dog, small dog, tough dog, scared dog, young dog, old dog—place any one of them next to a sick or dying man, let his hand touch that fur, and watch the miracle.

A recent video by The Latham Foundation (Alameda, California, 94501) depicts the multitudinous roles dogs play in the lives of HIV-infected patients, who are often shunned by family and friends. As one man says on film, "I came home sick last night and told Nick, my dog, I just didn't feel well . . . then I laid on the floor. Nick gave me a wet kiss and placed his head on my body. It meant so much to me. For there is no human in my life who can do that for me."

I forget where it was. The newspaper reported a boy was comatose; neither Mom nor Dad could pull him out. The boy was gone, and he'd been gone a long time. Mute and motionless and scarcely breathing. Then someone thought of bringing in the boy's dog. The moment the boy touched Pup's fur, his eyes twitched, his fingers fumbled, and if you looked real close, you could see the rebirth of a long-lost smile. The boy lived.

WHY THIS BOOK?

I know dogs. I live dogs. I love dogs. Those are my credentials, and I want to give all I've learned and felt and sensed to you. Especially

Blessed are the children when Granddad owns a kennel.

how to *communicate* with this new member of your family and fathom his nature. And simple things, like how to feed your dog, spot sickness, pick a vet, and avoid tinkling in the house.

But more than that, I want to hand you the keys to Pup's psyche so you can read the dog and know what he's going to do before he does it. I want to sensitize you so you can feel and appreciate Pup's gift: to lower your blood pressure, drain your tension, extend your life, and, when all people and all things have failed you, to give you something you must care for and thus get up the cheerful gumption to take on each new day as it comes.

But I've got more than that to offer. My wife Dee and I are a childless couple (61 percent of pet-owning households have no children living at home) and our house dogs are Dee's children.

Dee's relationship with her dogs mirrors the in-house realities of millions of American households. So in this book you'll find this trainer's no-nonsense, work-dog-proven training knowledge, plus Dee's extraordinary insight into pups because of her strong maternal instinct and unlimited love. Consequently, we'll not only have your pup coming on request, but we'll also have him tinkling in the yard, eating his nummy-nummy, and going nighty-night ('cause that's how Dee talks, and now she's got me doing it).

I love Dee and you will, too. Nothing delights her more than getting the monthly issue of a magazine she's had addressed to Chili Tarrant, one of her Lhasas. Or having a vet hold one of her pooches and sing "Happy Birthday" to it. Or having friends hand-make doodad gifts to put under the tree at Christmas for her family of kids.

And don't go thinking Dee is some fantasy-fetched gal who would skip through the tulips with Alice in Wonderland. Dee is a veteran business executive who oversees scores of associates in the full-court-press world of a women's clothing chain. She's basic and battle-forged in all things except her dogs—there, I admit, she is loving as a lamb and defensive as a hawk.

The first moments of a love-trained pup.

The Love-Trained Dog

Now I'm going to introduce you to the new world of the love-trained dog, where a bonded dog will respond to your scowl of disappointment with more pain than if you'd knocked him down with a two-by-four.

Where we'll train with facial expressions, body language, tone of voice, odor (yes, odor), intimacy, and mutual respect.

Where we'll never lift our voice or our hand.

With a Dog There's Always a Predicament

I'm standing at the sink now pulling skin off chicken breasts. I had to drive all over town to find what the doctor ordered. Most breasts had the rib bones intact, or they were immersed in what was called a "3% Baste." Just pure, no-bone, no-skin chicken breasts is what I was told to get. To mix with rice. "Anything else," said Doc, "and you'll blow her kidney." For Muffy is an older dog, and one kidney is gone.

Anyway, I'm pulling the skin from this chicken and the rice is boiling while I'm thinking of the wonder of this sick dog whose life has blessed mine. Yesterday I had her at the vet for a saline flush to dump the poison from her bloodstream and her kidney. As I was leaving, the vet handed me a one-eyed rabbit.

A guy had brought the bunny in asking if it had an eye beneath that pinch-closed eyelid. The vet looked and said no. Then the guy said, "Well, that's a genetic trait and she'll pass it along, so put her to sleep."

But the vet asked if the bunny could be kept and given away, and the man said yes. So when I showed up, the vet pushed the bunny into my hands and told me to scoot.

THE BEGINNING OF THE MIRACLES

I housed the bunny in a kennel crate in the living room while I fixed the house pack's dinner (Dee's on the road). Then, when everyone was settled, I reached in and got the rabbit and presented it to the family of dogs—holding the rabbit so it couldn't struggle and set off an emotional whirlwind—when Puddin, a one-year-old Lhasa apso, leaned forward, and gently, so gently, licked the bunny's missing eye.

I was stunned. How did Puddin know this spot was the infirmity? How did she know that if anything hurt, it would be there? I couldn't believe it.

But why not? That's the compassion and sensitivity and phenomenal insight and empathy I see dogs display every day.

For remember: God gave dogs all the virtues He said man should have but doesn't: qualities like goodness, faithfulness, trust, forbearance, love, steadfastness. You know the list!

Happy-faced Tiffy gets close to the one-eyed bunny. This bunny proved to be ecstasy for the pack.

THE DAILY DRAMA

We didn't know Punk was dying. She went down the porch steps and did her business and came back up and walked to the far side of the porch and lay down. But Sugar went to her and put her throat over the back of Punky's neck. We glanced at this behavior for a while, then went to bed.

The next morning, Punk was dead of a stroke. How did Sugar sense Punky's death the night before? I shared my daily life with Punky for fifteen years. I knew her backward and forward, but I missed her most important message. Why? Because what Punky communicated to Sugar was ineffable. And that's what dogs do so well. They send and interpret signs that are incomprehensible to a human being.

THE SHEPHERD WHO KNEW WHAT THE FAMILY DIDN'T

Kate, an old shepherd bitch, lived in a house with a middle-aged couple and the wife's mother. The couple worked and came home late at night, barely saw the mother for supper, then rushed off to work the next morning.

But on weekends they began to notice Kate's strange behavior. Every time Grandma approached a wall or piece of furniture or went close to the basement door, Kate blocked her path. There was no doubt Kate was overstepping her bounds, and if she wasn't careful, she could very easily trip the old lady.

Then one Sunday it all became clear. The husband asked for cauliflower, and Grandma passed him potatoes. The elderly woman was going blind—and only Kate knew. Kate had been protecting the woman for months when the couple didn't have a clue.

THE CANINE THERAPIST

Ever had diabetes? You can get a strange feeling from it. There comes a breathlessness—a sickness you can't pinpoint. It's a general malaise:

Without his dog, this cyclist wouldn't enter the parade.

You want to eat, you want to sleep, you want to get home fast because you think you may die in the street.

Well, Bob Region of Alexandria, Louisiana, was an active outdoorsman who got bad diabetes. Got it bad enough that a depression set in that nullified any desire Bob had to live. Even his wife Linda felt she was failing as a helpmate.

But Pepper, the family's female Lab, who often hunted with Bob, sensed the man's gloom and began dispensing her own kind of cure. She'd display on the floor, making funny sounds and movements, and she enticed Bob to get down there to play and tussle with her. Then, later, the two of them took walks in the field, and finally they hunted once more.

Today Bob is managing his diabetes, he's happy, and both Linda and Bob acknowledge their debt to the canine therapist named Pepper.

A GIFT FOR ETERNITY

There was an unlikely family of Mom and Dad, a mongrel cocker bitch named Allie, and a potbellied pig named Amy. Allie and Amy were a delight to each other. They played, they talked to each other, they slept together. Allie the dog ate pig starter, and Amy the pig ate dog food.

Then it happened. Amy walked out on the pool cover one day. The side of the canvas dipped beneath the water, and Amy went under to drown. When Las Vegans Pat and Richard Heymann came home from work that night, in grief and horror they pulled Amy from the pool, laid her on the deck, and sat beside her, crying.

Allie was five years old, and in all her years, she had a favorite possession, without which she was seldom seen. It was a little green rubber frog. Allie walked over to stand above Amy and, lowering her head, rolled the little green frog out to the pig as a final gift. That night, when Amy was removed for burial, Allie did not take back her frog. It was a gift for eternity.

Give a Miracle to Get a Miracle

But sometimes a dog's contribution is not so apparent. Take the case of Daisy. In the town of Cornelius, Oregon, there was a spirited old lady named Henrietta who was a walking ray of sunshine, making her rounds each morning on the town's sidewalks, gladdening all she met, while out front galloped Daisy, the gap-toothed, pampas-grass-tailed, scruffy white dog.

Rain or shine the duo appeared, ever smiling, ever cheering, ever enjoying their lives with each other and all they met.

Then one day Henrietta did not appear. And another. Still another. And the townspeople grew concerned, so some went to check and found Henrietta in a darkened room with a dying dog. Daisy was fog-eyed, her tongue protruding blue and limp between gapped teeth, her tousled coat without sheen.

These people who cared about Henrietta and Daisy insisted the dog be taken to the vet. The dog must be checked. For now it was revealed to the townspeople that Daisy was the generator of Henrietta's life.

Daisy was delivered to Dr. Bob Bullard, a middle-aged, soft-haired, casual-appearing but extremely precise and competent vet, who made an emergency examination. What he learned was serious. Daisy's ailment could be fatal, the treatment was costly, and Henrietta was without money—that's why she hadn't brought Daisy in.

Doc admits Daisy to the hospital and starts emergency medical care. Daisy will have to stay. So Henrietta trudges home with empty heart: spiritless, grave, without hope.

When next morning through the clinic door with a burst of self-purpose comes a middle-aged woman who tells the doc, "Pleased to meet you. I'm Henrietta's daughter . . . just come up from California when I heard about Daisy."

The woman slips off her gloves, removes her coat. "Do you think the dog will live?" she asks the doc.

And he turns to her with grave concern, for he's heard more in her question than what she's expressed. "Why do you ask?" he inquires.

Dr. Bob Brullard takes time out with a brace of English springer spaniels.

"Because if Daisy would die, it really would be for the best. Mother is much too old to be up here in this wet Oregon weather gallivanting all around. With Daisy gone, we could convince Mom to come to California and live in a nursing home . . . give up this foolish independence . . . it would be better really. So much better." She hesitates a moment, then asks, "Couldn't Daisy just pass away?" Then, stammering, "It would relieve Daisy of all her pain and suffering."

Doc looks at the cold steel examining table and thinks of what will happen to Henrietta in a bureaucratic, regimented environment with most of her self-determination denied. Then he says in a determined voice, "Well, you'll need an excuse other than Daisy dying to take your mother away . . . for Daisy is going to live a very long time."

Then the intense vigil begins: all the doctoring and care and prayer. But something extraordinary is happening. By word of mouth, Cornelius has learned of Henrietta's fate, and small amounts of money are coming in to pay a bill Bullard never intended to send. There are lighted prayer candles at altars. And Sunday mornings the veterinarian leaves his family and the horses he loves and the springer spaniels he walks with in the fields and goes to Daisy's kennel, scootches down to sit on the concrete kennel run, and hand-feeds Daisy with love and a beseeching voice.

You're right. It took a long time, but Daisy lived, and Henrietta kissed her daughter good-bye. The following week, Cornelius saw the sun shine again. For down the walk came Henrietta and the little white fluff named Daisy.

A vet hadn't just saved a dog, he'd saved a woman as well, and lifted the spirits of his community. For Cornelius—with all that Oregon rain—would still have that ray of sunshine named Henrietta come passing by, propelled by a little white dog called Daisy.

So what's the moral of this story? If you bring your dogs into your home and heart, they'll bond as each of these dogs did, and you'll witness miracles you never imagined.

Let's start bonding. It all begins on the next page.

2

Scent Makes Sense

We know the dog's primary trait as a lover of humans, but a biologist might say a dog exists for the sole and express purpose of carrying his nose.

United States Border Patrol: Nogales, Arizona

We're in the tumbledown town of Nogales, Arizona, at a border-patrol check station where two hundred eighteen-wheelers snort through each day hauling fresh produce to the States. We see a smudged and dented semi appear between the tiers of cascading huts. Loaded with nine tons of fresh green onions, the truck chugs to a stop at the inspection station.

A dog named Lobo walks up, takes a sniff, and tells his handler, "It's here." Customs Officer Douglas Toenjes and Lobo dig down through the pungent cargo and find ten grams of cocaine. That's .0353 ounce (approximately one-third the weight of a copper penny). Found in nine tons of slimy, wet, stinking green onions.

UNITED STATES BORDER PATROL: CASA GRANDE, ARIZONA

Casa Grande, Arizona, sits on the interstate between Tucson and Phoenix amid a dusty patchwork of cotton fields. The primary rural residents are Colorado River toads (if a dog licks one, he can die) and rattlesnakes.

Late one night, a semi eases into town, the driver moseying about, eventually stopping. One by one, dark figures appear from the neighborhood. Everyone laughs nervously at their success. Then the trap is sprung, and a cadre of officers surrounds the truck. Intelligence told them what was coming.

Border Patrol Officer "Big Ed" Heitschmidt tells us, "I went in with my dog and told him, 'Find it,' as I started him on the downwind corner of the big truck. When we got to the saddle tank, he alerted. Right through the steel, right through a hundred or so gal-

A German shorthair sniffing for drugs may be onto something.

lons of diesel fuel, he alerted. So we got in there, and immersed in the fuel and wrapped in aluminum foil and cellophane and aluminum foil and cellophane, over and over, then wrapped in a burlap bag and taped to the bottom of the tank, we found two pounds of heroin."

United States Border Patrol: Otay Mesa, California

Otay Mesa is a U.S. Customs cargo facility built in 1985 some eight miles south of San Ysidro. Export-import businesses have sprung up about the government facility, and sixty-four hundred people now live there. But still, Otay Mesa is a desolate place of forlorn, detached, and hard-packed barrens.

On this particular day, twenty to twenty-five semis with tankers equipped to haul propane pull up in two lines. Canine Enforcement Officer Jeff Weitzman starts down one line with his forty-eight-pound Labrador-mix bitch, appropriately named Snag. She's sniffing the tires and tanks and running boards when suddenly she pivots and lunges, literally hurtling her handler across the road to the opposite line of trucks. At the third truck down, which hauls an empty propane tanker, Snag sings out in body language, "We've got it."

What happened? The truck entered Mexico, dumped its propane, and is now returning empty. But in the meantime, someone has secreted cocaine in the tank—but through the steel and the pungency of propane, Snag alerts. Propane is odorless, but ethylmercaptan, a safety additive, emits a horrible stench.

It takes twenty-four hours to bleed off the fumes and enter the tank (propane being explosive), whereupon customs officers find 8,705 pounds of cocaine with an estimated street value of $564 million—the largest seizure of cocaine ever made at a land-border port of entry.

SO WHAT'S OUR BOX SCORE?

Cocaine in onions, heroin in diesel fuel, cocaine in ethylmercaptan. Plus, here's more!

A mixed Lab named Shoe found 7,083 pounds of marijuana secreted in jalapeño peppers.

Golden retriever Shane found TNT in a hidden safe.

And Labrador Tattoo found seventy-two thousand pounds of marijuana buried beneath tons of gravel on a cargo ship.

None of these masking agents was strong enough to evade these sniff-dogs' noses. So throughout this book you must remember this: *There is nothing on earth so sensitive and dynamic as a dog's nose.* It is miraculous; it is unfathomable.

You and I walk into a kitchen and smell chili on the stove. The dog walks in and smells cumin, oregano, coriander, chili powder—even water.

Only if you remember this trait will you partially understand the dog. Only if you honor this power will you begin to gain the slightest inkling into how the dog interprets his world. However, the nose is not the dog's primary sensor, as we shall see. There's a dog secret few know. A phenomenon few people have ever imagined. We will discover it in chapter 3.

THE NOSE KNOWS

Man has no sense comparable to a dog's nose. Call your dog, and he'll show you how it works. Take a tidbit pressed between your index finger and thumb and extend it to Pup. Does he snatch it? No. He smells it. And why is this? Is it because he's finicky? Because he's suspicious? No. It's because this is how dogs taste.

So much in a dog's world is based on smell.

Dee follows me to bed at night: She's a hoot owl. So here she comes with those six Lhasa apsos, who scramble on the bed and come bounding up to smell my head protruding from the covers. I know Dee's faithful, or I'd wonder who the hell's been sleeping in my place to prompt the dogs to check each night. But smelling is seeing to these dogs—and every other dog. Remember this. Do not forget this. It's the basis of a ton of dog behavior.

Should you doubt me, then do this tomorrow night. When you arrive home from work, come in from the garage all hunched over and walk with a limp. Your dogs will erupt in pandemonium. You don't fit the fuzzy pattern they usually see. (More about eyesight later.) Not until one dog from the pack sneaks up behind and smells you will the rest relax.

ONE DOG CONFIRMS FOR ALL

This is because dogs confirm for one another. While gathering source material in Africa, I'd come upon packs of fifty wild African hunting dogs, *Lycaon pictus,* taking the morning sun. Hidden from their scent and hearing and view, I'd wait and watch. Suddenly,

Wild hunting dogs sit like bookends to monitor their world.

though I had sensed nothing, all fifty heads would come up at the same time. It seems in the world of dogs what one dog senses they all sense. And did they do this with their noses?

Take a pack of wolves on the trail of caribou. Or just take two wolves working in concert. Wolves totally out of sight of each other—yet moving in unison, each probing to drive the caribou toward the other—will checkmate the caribou's path. Could they have done this with nose alone?

The Invisible Rubber Band

Or take Mike Gould of The Flying B Ranch in Kamiah, Idaho. I've stood on a hill and watched Mike work his miracle Labrador retriever named Web with what Mike calls the "invisible rubber band." Web and Mike cannot see each other; but when Mike backs up, Web comes in; when Mike goes forward, Web backs up; when Mike turns right, Web turns left.

Mike and Web have bonded. Henceforth always remember bonding. We'll talk about this a lot. And that's what wild hunting dogs, or any dogs, do. They bond and have one brain, one heart, one intent, which makes possible one identical interpretation of senses and one identical solution.

The only problem here is that Mike and Web are so far apart—with a hill between them (and the wind is not blowing from Mike to Web)—that Web cannot smell Mike. So how does Web decode Mike's actions? What does Web sense? Is something else triggering Web's behavior? Have an idea what this is? I do.

There is another dimension. The dog does not live by scent alone. As miraculous as the dog's nose is—there is more to the dog than his nose.

3

Scent or ESP?

My wife Dee's at the age when she's having hot flashes. I mention this and she erupts in a huff for, with her, these words take on more meaning than I assign to them. Then she tells me what she's really having are power surges. Funny how communication can become so complicated. It sure does in training a pup. As we shall see.

I've thought mightily, and written much, about the phenomenal scenting ability of dogs, and I think it is all best illustrated by Joe Simpson of Danville, California. This one-of-a-kind trainer of police dogs, retrievers, and border collies is called on for research by universities. Unbeknownst to each other, both Stanford and Duke once contracted Joe to conduct an experiment for the Department of Defense.

You see, it was during the Vietnam War, and though we had secretly developed an instrument that would stop a Jeep approaching a land mine, it wouldn't work when the mine was under water.

So Joe tells me Duke figured a dog would detect the mine by extrasensory perception (ESP: a Duke research specialty). But Stanford said, "Oh, no, if they detect it at all, they will smell it." For here's what's at stake. If the dogs smell the land mine that is under water, then scientists can build a machine based on the olfactory process to stop vehicles short of running over water-covered land mines. That means saving the lives of lots of soldiers. However, if the dogs detect the mines through ESP, then no science yet exists to invent a contraption to trigger on nebulously transmitted thought processes (or whatever's at work here). So the two universities asked Joe to train his dogs on underwater "shoe" mines, and Joe worked several dogs in a shallow backyard swimming pool for many months.

THE ULTIMATE TEST

Then one day the experiment was conducted on a Pacific beach. Boiled, sterile glass ashtrays were buried in a trench dug with a backhoe by personnel wearing boiled, sterile "space suits," and then the tide washed over the filled-in excavation several times. (The reason for this is because disturbed earth has a distinct odor to a dog. So the disturbed earth became one continuous filled-in trench, not separate holes the dogs could detect.) Everyone was convinced the tide would wash away the scent of the freshly dug trench.

Then off in the distance some mathematicians—who knew where each glass ashtray was buried—monitored Joe and each successive dog as they walked the "mine" field.

Each time a dog would alert on a glass ashtray, Joe would stick a small flagpole into the ground. After Joe took several walks with different dogs, the mathematicians, who were reading equipment that recorded exactly where each "mine" was buried, reported Joe's dogs were successful in detecting 77 percent of the boiled, sterile glass ashtrays. Read that again and think about it: That percentage is absolutely phenomenal.

"Hooray," said Duke, "this proves what we've said all along. It was impossible for the dogs to smell those ashtrays—yet they knew where they were. So they had to trigger by ESP."

"Bosh," said Stanford. "The handler didn't bury the glass ashtrays.

He didn't know where they were. So how could he have transmitted a thought process about something he didn't know? Now we're convinced the dogs really did smell the buried ashtrays."

The two universities argued, then finally turned to Joe and asked, "So tell us, just how did your dogs do it?"

And Joe, who had been with the army K-9 Corps and gone behind enemy lines—what was it?—over one hundred times and then trained attack dogs for the underworld (yes, he did) and finally ended up on San Francisco television teaching viewers how to train their house dogs, looked at his puzzled sponsors and said, "Hell, I don't know."

Now here's the bottom line. The opposing scientists with Joe that day thought either dogs might scent boiled, "odorless" glass ashtrays, or trigger on any nuance our bodies emit as a result of thought stimulation (ESP). Neither theory was proved, however, since Joe had no idea where the ashtrays were buried, and he figured it would be hard to conclude that he cued the dogs mentally.

When We Think, We Stink

But why didn't any of the scholars figure the dogs might smell Joe's detection of the buried "targets"? During their evolution, dogs have adapted smelling cells extremely sensitive to odors that relate to peril, food gathering, perpetuation of the species—anything that means life or death. Of importance here is the dog's phenomenal recognition of butyric acid, found in human sweat. Tests show that dogs smell human sweat one million times better than humans do. And it's stunning to learn that the average adult sweats a quart a day. And dogs also discriminate between smells given off by our natural skin oils and a complex of gaseous components created by what we eat, touch, breathe, and wear—everything from shoes to booze.

When our body is aroused, then, it emits subtle odors a dog can scent. And should Joe have "felt" the presence of a buried ashtray, his body would have announced that fact to a dog.

Now, I neither speak for Duke nor Stanford—these are my interpretations, not theirs. But what Duke was apparently hanging its hat on was this: It does seem that dogs can read our minds. For example, is that what's happening with Web beyond the hill when he knows every time Mike changes direction and which way he steps?

But could it possibly be there are two other things happening? Either dogs interpret our thoughts through scent, or they learn us so well that they can predict our thoughts and resultant actions through seemingly imperceptible stimuli.

Thus, if dogs *can* read our minds, I submit they do it, at least partially—and preferably at close range—with their noses. For unbeknownst to us, some thoughts we have may trigger the emission of odors. *When we think, we stink.* I offer anxiety as an example: When we're uptight, we do sweat.

So let's back up to Joe and his mine dogs. If Joe had known where the mines were buried, his body would have shown excessive emotion at each location, and this could have been transmitted by body odor: Remember, a quart of sweat a day, and dogs trigger especially on butyric acid—plus a thousand emitted gaseous compounds.

But here's something the scientists didn't factor into their test. Since these mathematicians knew where each glass ashtray was buried, and since dogs can smell in excess of a hundred yards, could it be Joe's dogs were smelling the aroused emotions of the scientists? Wouldn't these personnel become tense when each dog approached a buried, boiled glass ashtray? Certainly they would. So what way was the wind blowing? From the scientists toward the dogs? For me, that would answer it.

In any experiment, the scientist must eliminate all extraneous variables, and maybe this is one variable the team forgot to isolate and control.

COMMUNICATION

What's involved in all of this is communication. Pure and simple. And that's what's involved in all dog training. For all training is based on three requirements: repetition, point of contact, and association.

Let me explain. We repeat the training lesson over and over—that's repetition. To control the dog—especially the large working dog—we have a point of contact, which is usually a collar about the dog's neck that's connected to a leash. And finally, there's association. Pull the leash and say, "Come here." Finally the dog associates the physical tug on his collar with the verbal command "come here."

But in this book we're going to minimize touching our dog in training. So our point of contact has to be our voice, touching Pup's eardrums. Or our disappointed face glimpsed by Pup's eyes. Or our emitted odor of disappointment—or triumph. Risky? Not really. We'll get the job done. But first I must ask for your indulgence and your patience. Read on.

4

FIDO

There is something beyond our knowledge
that is found between man and dog.

Communication means that which is shared equally by two or more. Communication is the basis of all dog–man relationships, and all dog training.

Now to share something equally is nearly impossible. For example, the Eskimo and I both speak English. Fine, you say, you can communicate. Can we? I say "dog" and the picture in the Eskimo's head is a husky, but I was thinking of an English pointer. We did not share everything equally. We did not communicate.

Dog–Man Communication

All training is communication that results in changed behavior. And though communication seems simple, it is very complex. The many components include a sender, code, channel, receiver, and so on.

Also, to accomplish complete communication, both sender and receiver must send and receive feedback. And when this feedback is taken to the nth degree—is that what we call ESP? That is the ability to share each other's emotions or feelings—and probably much, much more.

The model I use for feedback is FIDO: which means the man is FILLING IN and DIGGING OUT a dog's response to a message.

Plus, a dog is doing the same with a man.

Our Model

Now what do I mean by "filling in"? Well, the man is communicating to the dog, but the dog looks confused. That means not everything is clear. Which further means there are flaws in the message. It's that simple. So the man keeps communicating until all the flaws are dug out and filled in—correctly.

Movement

And how do you know the flaws exist? Because you can read the dog. There will be much more about this in later chapters. But to read a dog you look for nuances in body movement, such as the arch of the tail, the cock of the ears, tenseness in the shoulder muscles, a bowed neck.

Such telltale movements include:

1. a dog taking several rapid steps forward tells you he's trying to figure out something in the distance
2. a dog pawing your ankle means he wants your attention (this was his first physical communication in trying to gain the attention of his mother)
3. spinning in rapid circles means the dog's delighted with the upcoming prospects—such as your lowering his food bowl, reaching down to put him in the car, or getting ready to throw a ball

4. a large dog standing or sitting with a paw on your foot is trying to gain dominance over you

5. when the dog's tail drops while working, he's telling you he's tired. And on and on.

A Dog's Expression

Or you look for changes in expression. These can be slitted or blinking eyes, dilated nostrils, drooped ears, a smacking of dry lips. For example, if a dog should appear sick in the eyes, this indicates he's not happy with the idleness of the hour—he wants something to happen.

Also, if a dog's shoulder and leg muscles relax and he takes a swallow, this is the sign that he's "sighing." It means he's given in momentarily to whatever you want him to do. When he's sighed three times, he's forgone all resistance. He's accepted your lesson.

Purposely turning his eyes away from you means the dog's mad at you. If his eyes are turned away and slitted, the dog is afraid of you.

When the dog's head is down, his eyes are dull, and his shoulders are drooped, he's telling you he's sick.

When his jowls are wrinkled, his teeth bared, his eyes glaring, and his tail wagging in short, stiff beats, the dog's angry at another dog.

If a dog looks at you and then somewhere else over and over, it means he wants you to take him that direction. Or he wants you to go inspect something, for instance, a noise at the front door.

The Talking Dog

Listen to what the dog has to say. Dogs have a great repertoire of sounds: whimpers, barks, growls, guttural purrs, scratches with the paws, and smackings of the mouth. Generally, these sounds are transmitted with both facial expressions and body movements. For example, a dog lying on his stomach with paws stretched forward is not in a submissive position but just taking it easy. But should the

Dee sits to talk with her brood. She's looking at Puddin. To Puddin's left, Sugar tells Puddin to go away. Beneath Dee's extended arm, Tiffy looks back in disapproval of Chili's getting any loving. Candy stands before them all and wants everyone to leave so she can have Dee to herself. I'd say that's communication enough.

dog begin smiling, then scooting forward by placing one outstretched paw before the other, and purring, then that dog is begging. If a dog has been scolded, this animation also means he wants you to accept him once again.

A dog standing on his hind legs and barking usually means "yes," or "let's do it." Or it can also be an enthusiastic greeting if the dog is also whining, licking, doing the twist, and laughing.

Finally, if the dog is growling, flicking his tongue like a snake, and turning his head sideways so you get a great flash of white from his eyes, this dog is telling you he's mighty damned mad, and either knock it off or get away.

These movements, sounds, and expressions are the cues from which you dig out feedback. They tell you if you're getting anywhere. They tell you where the flaws are.

But the ultimate sign to read for flaws in communication is found in the dog's eyes. And there's no way to tell you what to look for; it comes only after years of recognizing the unique expression of your dog's eyes and the accompanying behavior. I can tell you that a dog's eyes express all those things found in humans: joy, sorrow, anger, illness, rejection, desire—but here's the catch—a dog's eyes can express much, much more. Something you'll know at an instant but have no name for. Not now, not ever. Such eyes express a meaning you come to know by faith. Like I know when a dog's telling me, "You've got to be kidding." But there's no way I can tell you what I'm seeing.

When Communication Doesn't Work

Let's say we've asked a mature dog to come. He balks. We get down on one knee and he still refuses to move. We pose gleefully and clap our hands, sweeten our voice. We whistle. A whistle startles a dog: He will jerk about to look.

But the dog has made up his mind to refuse us. In other words, the desired performance is for the dog to come, but each successive communication proves worthless. We cannot remove and correct the flaws: We cannot communicate. For remember, we communicate to achieve modified behavior, and this dog ain't coming.

So what do we do now? If we start toward this dog, he'll run away. So we leave our jacket as a scent post and come back later. The dog may eventually come to the coat and lie there. The familiar assurance of your odor may keep him there until you return.

So how good a trainer you really are—meaning how well you can read and think dog—determines whether the dog will ever come.

But how did this balking dog come about? I'll tell you. This dog was lost for several days, and many such dogs are so frightened when they're finally found that they won't even come to their human partner.

Out of fear and uncertainty, the dog has shut out all communication. So we go to his primary sensor—his nose—leave the area, and know the dog will be drawn to the odor that previously meant love and care and assurance.

Digging Out

So what about the trainer digging out the dog's response? Well, what we're talking about here is the man's good senses deciphering everything the dog is displaying in response to his message.

And this may be very subtle. For that reason, we often say that a good dog trainer has "the gift." Nobody knows what the gift is, but essentially it means this man knows more than most other men about how to communicate to and interpret the feedback from a dog. The reason this is so hard to describe—this gift—is that the dog responds to touch, smell, taste, sound, and, I believe, ESP. There'll be several examples of "the gift" as we journey through this book. The gift is as hard to fathom as is the ability of a dog to detect one-third of an ounce of cocaine in nine tons of green onions.

But said simply, to *dig out* means the trainer sensitizes himself to maximum perception of clues the dog gives back in response to the trainer's message.

The human partner with the lost dog knew this. Knew the dog was so frightened he wouldn't come. So the man left, leaving the motivation up to the dog. For as Delmar Smith, the Okie dog pro who has the gift, says, "The come has got to be in the dog . . . not in you." If you decipher that statement, you're well on your way to becoming a dog trainer, because I think Delmar is half-dog.

How It's Done

The man and the dog (even the newborn pup relating to its mother) exchange messages. They interact. First it's touch and smell, but there is also transmitted feeling. Hold the pup close to your cheek, and he will fold into you and make a soft whimper-panting sound. He responds to the communication of your warmth and touch and odor, and what else? The closer you hold him, the more secure he becomes. For pups are very frightened of falling. That's why if a pup throws a tantrum (and some males will), just hold him straight out with all four feet dangling and let him peer down. He'll become a pacifist pronto.

From the beginning, dog and man share each other's feelings and emotions. But only slightly at first, as I show in this illustration. The child picks up the puppy by his tail, and the puppy screams. The child has hurt the pup. The pup interprets this act as one of willfully inflicting pain. He wants nothing to do with this child.

But the man picks up the puppy and holds it to his cheek, or the woman places the pup upon her breast, and the pup feels the warmth of the body, the tenderness of the hands. He smells the acceptance the human holds for him. He senses the pleasure, the tenderness, the love.

For a dog, that's the ultimate test: hurt or love. All dog–man relationships are built on this one fact. Matter of fact, much psychological theory is based on this: It is called reward or punishment.

Later, when dog and man have bonded, the feelings (or messages) become very complex and quite subtle. And the greater the love, which means the greater the bonding, the greater the unspoken communication between them. Like a human couple married fifty years: The man's reading his paper and his wife says, "Bring me a cup, too." The man's not surprised. It's been happening for years. The way she reads his mind. The way she knew he was going for a cup of coffee before he ever moved.

A Better Understanding

Ever know of a witcher? That's a guy who takes a forked willow- or fruit-tree stick and, holding one fork in each fist, extends his arms and walks along, pointing the end of the stick straight out, with his palms up. The base of the fork must be six inches, and each of the forks at least eighteen inches long. The witcher may also hold a piece of brass in his right hand.

So here he comes. When the six-inch section starts to pull down, the witcher drops the piece of brass to the ground and continues walking. When the entire branch—both forks and pointer—goes to ground, the witcher sticks the pointer into the earth. Then he walks back to where he dropped the piece of brass. Let's say that's twenty-six feet. Thereupon he turns to the well driller and tells him, "Drill where I stuck that stick in the ground, and you'll hit water at twenty-six feet."

The driller drills and hits water at twenty-six feet.

The terms used for the witcher's ability are "diving" or "dousing." And there's no way to explain what we're witnessing than to say it's an act of God.

All of this composes an extraordinary communication between a stick and an underground stratum of water; or a man and the water; or man, stick, and water; or whatever you might consider.

And this suggests something else for our dog–man communication model. When taken to the nth degree, could this also be an act of God?

So Much for Science

I was a freshman taking a geology course on the GI Bill when I saw my first witcher. I witnessed the man's success—but this could not be! For my geology professor had instilled in me the scientific process. Which means you must be able to explain the cause and effect of any physical result. You must be able to explain (or, better yet, measure) how things occur.

So I rushed to him, bursting open his office door, and stuttering out my discovery and disbelief. I said to him, "That can't actually happen, can it?"

And the professor—I remember his name was Berg—looked at me with a wearied expression and said, "Don't bet against it."

"But how can it happen?" I blurted. "There is no visible cause and effect."

He told me, "Science can go so far . . . then you encounter things beyond explanation. But," he added, "witchers can find water when a geologist can't. And we don't know how it's done."

So those of you who want to know how dog and man communicate remember FIDO: the filling in and digging (or is it divining?) out the thoughts and emotions of the other. I can assure you it happens. I can also assure you we haven't the slightest idea of how it occurs. It's as real—and as baffling—as witching water.

Is it something, then, that we must take on faith? The way Dr. Berg accepted the witcher?

Pups Sense Feeling. Remember This!

Pups have not yet learned language. So they must respond to *feelings* we transmit, and we have to adjust our "messages" by reading how the pup's responding. In other words, we're feeling, too. We call this feedback. It's played like a mental Ping-Pong game.

So what happens can be modeled like this: The man and the pup exchange feelings—which are converted by each into a reaction. Whatever the reaction is—that is, whatever the receiver shows upon receipt of the message—is read and decoded by the sender. This prompts the sender to either sustain the same message or modify it to get the desired response. Which means the adjustment in communication is sustained until the man and dog have reached a common ground. Or to say it another way: to have reached that state where something is shared equally by two or more.

Responding To Telepathy

Let me give you a stunning example of man–dog communication. Jim Charlton of Sauvie Island, in Portland, Oregon, is a custom trainer of golden retrievers. This six-feet-six, antenna-stretched man with the soft voice, gentle hands, and a philosopher's bent, was visiting the home of a client one day. Casey, the dog Jim had trained, was lying across the room.

Jim said to the dog's human partner, "I can make Casey come to me and not say a word."

"Ho-ho," exclaimed the man, "that would be a trick."

So Jim sat in the chair, did not look at Casey, but in his mind kept saying over and over, "Casey, come here. Casey, come here."

Casey gradually stood, walked to Jim, and laid his head on the trainer's near leg.

You tell me what happened.

Becoming Verbal

Pups gradually do learn spoken words; they do learn language. So now we need another communication model. It goes like this.

The dog now responds to what he knows, not just what he feels. For now he knows language. He also knows how language is transmitted: loudly, softly, happily, angrily, teasingly, and so on. Therefore, what is our complete communication model for training?

The sender transmits both knowledge (the dog understands language) and emotion. It's sent over one of a number of channels: sight, sound, taste, touch, smell. Which means the dog trainer must be especially sensitive and attentive. He must always be trying to understand the dog. This is imperative. Take the professional trainers on the hunting-dog circuit. Many make the dog fit their system. Too many of these dogs are scuttled. But the successful trainers create a system to bring along the uniqueness of each dog. Sensitivity—that's the imperative.

The mature dog, the dog in advanced training, continues to respond to what he learned about man as a puppy, be that from body posture, odor, language, facial expression, body heat, ESP. But now the dog also knows language. So the mature dog is also reacting to the words themselves—even if someone other than you is saying them. The dog's responding to what those words have meant in the past. That's why any man can handle another man's trained dog: the dog knows the words of command.

THE WORDS OF COMMAND MAY NOT BE WORDS AT ALL

I recall the story about Freeman Lloyd, the Welshman who was gundog editor of *Field & Stream* for forty-eight years. He was one of a group that captured a lioness in South Africa for the zoo Cecil Rhodes gave to the citizens of London. Down at the docks that night, while loading the big cat, the rope broke, the crate fell, and Katrina (the lioness) leaped out of the exploding splinters.

Freeman was so startled—and remember he was a dog man—that instinctively he boomed in a loud, commanding voice, "Katrina, kennel!" (which is the command to get a dog into an enclosure). Whereupon, it is authenticated, Katrina jumped back into the debris of her destroyed crate—and sat there.

With tongue in cheek, I could tell you Katrina knew the words of command. But never before had this wild cat heard them in her jungle haunts. Yet hear them this time she did, and knowing what they meant (not from language, but from the presence of the man, from his impossible and ridiculously baseless dominance), she leaped back from whence she had come. And though it was a big cat—that, my friends, was dog handling.

All of which goes to say that whether or not the dog knows the words, it's the way the trainer says them, the way he sounds, the way he looks—even, in this case, his demanding presence—that gains compliance.

Double Whammy

There is another aspect of communication. As the sender transmits a word in hopes the receiver will react the right way, the sender also reacts to his own message. Suddenly the *word* may remind the man how stupid it is to yell "kennel" at a wild, runaway lion. But the impetuous bluff has been played and must be sustained. So, not only are we reading feedback from the receiver, but we are also reading it from our own message, from our own words. Had Freeman Lloyd been given more time to think, I don't know what he would have added. But it's likely he would just have shut his mouth and wet his pants.

The Emphasis Is Feelings

So what must be concluded is this: Pups sense meaning in us. They feel our intercommunications. And when they grow to be dogs, they know the words we use and know better yet the silent communication we've shown throughout the dog's life. Remember Casey and Mike's retriever Web.

Grief as a Message

Just tonight Dee and I came from the vet with Muffy. This is the first time the vet says we must put Muffy down: The catheters have blown three arteries; there's only one left for an emergency.

Dee has walked through the house distressed. She sits in the backyard, and all the dogs crowd about her: Sugar leaps to Dee's lap, kissing her arm.

Dee has communicated her sadness to all of them. She did this by feeling something inwardly, not by transmitting something purposely. And the dogs' sympathy for Dee shows they have received the message, and they are communicating back to her.

If you want to see something miraculously tender, just let a dog start to upchuck, or gasp, or squeal in pain, and the house pack will run to his side. They'll all extend their noses, arch their necks. Sometimes one of them will walk up to press her chest against the ailing dog, extending her head across the dog's upper neck. Everyone is tense. Everyone is concerned. No tail is wagging.

Put a dog on a table to doctor his ears, clip his nails, clean his eyes, and every dog in the house will come running, standing there anxiously, looking up. And this happens when the dog has made no outcry. Then, when the doctored dog is lowered to the floor, he is examined closely.

ONE MORE FACTOR

Dogs do not just decode language, but the whole of us. When they are puppies, you say, "Come here." But the pup does not know words. So what do you do? You get on one knee, you subordinate yourself. You speak in baby talk; your language is not so much in words as in an ingratiating voice. You pat the ground and wave your arms toward yourself, you are animated and entertaining.

Take the nine- and eleven-year-old brothers who were featured in a story out of Spokane, Washington. Cory and Jay Eisenmann adopted two deaf dalmatians. The boys knew a smattering of sign language used by deaf humans, so one boy would give the hand sign for "sit" while his brother pushed the dog's rump down.

The dalmatians learned many commands—even to the boys signing "go-car-ride." For when this hand sign is given, at least one dalmatian ends up sitting by the back door, ready to go.

So much for those who shout.

POODY

Dee and I lost an old mongrel terrier several years ago who had a vocabulary of some three hundred words. She was uncanny. You may not believe this, but Poody learned to spell. That's right. Dee and I would agree we were going out, so we'd spell out our intentions to throw Poody off track. Ha! Poody would be waiting at the back door.

I suspect most live-in dogs know something less than fifty words. Yet they can get by with knowing only a handful, for they're reading signs you send involuntarily, apart from any language code.

I don't have to tell Candy "come here" when I head out to the car. This Lhasa-Maltese knows I work barefooted, or in house slippers. So when I put on shoes, the footgear tells her "come here," for she ends up waiting at the back door to get in the car.

This is what I cannot emphasize enough: Dogs are decoding us all the time and we're not even aware of the cues (or the codes) we are sending.

Pooder and the author are caught talking in the garden by an unexpected photographer. (Photograph by Dee Tarrant.)

Candy waits (im)patiently for her chauffeur.

FEEDBACK

FIDO is nothing more than shared feedback. We ask. The dog complies. Or we yell, and the dog cowers. If he complies, we continue with the same tactic, same smile, same tone of voice. The dog is soothed by us and wants to please, so he complies, and on and on. If we yell, the dog is frightened and wants to escape. So we've got to change our message, heh?

THE NEW TRAINING PROGRAM

So our new training program is this: We train with our head, not our hand. We are always the friend of the dog, never the enemy. If the dog must have more severe correction, we let other dogs do it. Or we situate the dog so it will self-train in our absence. Nothing bad ever happens to a dog that he can associate with a human being. And that's the main thrust of what we're all about—humanity.

Simply stated, what we're talking about is individuals, be they canine or human, who either yield or remain independent in an unavoidable situation. And this could be the definition of education, or training. Maximize the feedback between sender and receiver, and you're assured the maximum yield. The receiver will remain independent only if he rejects you or your message. It's like the man who named his dog Herpes. The dog wouldn't heel. Old Herpes either wasn't getting the message or was rejecting the sender.

LOVE, SWEET LOVE

As far as I'm concerned, love, is the ultimate bonding agent. And that's what dogs do best: They love humans. So they bond through continual feedback, or FIDO. They bond so tightly, they eventually know us better than we know ourselves. At least I know they become so perceptive that they respond to messages we don't even know we're transmitting. Because remember: The message doesn't have to contain words. The message to a dog must contain feelings, as we will see throughout this book.

Webster's New World Dictionary tells us that intuition is the "ability to perceive and know things without conscious reasoning." For example, it is said that you can't fool a dog. If your dog doesn't like a stranger, then you'd be wise to be leery of him, too. A dog's evaluation of human character is seldom wrong. Every time I've failed to agree with my dog's opinion of a newcomer I've been taken. Dogs are very intuitive.

Well, it's obvious we could continue this conversation forever, but I hope I've made my point. When you deal with a dog, you are dealing with an unfathomable creature: sensitive, intuitive, and ineffably discerning.

I've known for a long time that I'm going to my grave without ever having really understood just what it is I've witnessed as I've studied dogs deciphering humans. It is mysterious, uncanny, unfathomable. For example, all our dogs are piled beneath my typing table. I rise to go to the john, and they don't move. But if I rise to go out the back door, they beat me to the screen. How do they know?

DEALING WITH A DUMB ANIMAL: US!

Now let me say this before we continue. There is a current fallacy made popular by an author, who says that the important thing in a dog's life is another dog. Bosh! If that were the case, the dog would never have left the wilderness.

No, the important thing in a dog's life is the human with whom he has bonded. And bonding is the result of FIDO. But how does the dog do it? Scent, ESP, a combination of both, or none of the above? Think with me, probe with me, as we visit throughout this book. There's something miraculous going on. We're looking at it, and we haven't a clue what we're seeing.

For centuries we've said the dog was a dumb animal.

Who's looking dumb now?

5

The Rest of the Dog

A woman paid a vet's groomer thirty dollars to bathe her poodle. When the vet told her the dog needed a parvo shot, she asked what it cost. The vet told her sixteen dollars. The lady replied she couldn't afford it. Apparently the value of her dog was only skin deep.

All dogs have an abhorrence: They do not want to be alone. When I sit on the bathroom stool, the dogs do not go outdoors and play. Being with another dog is not important to them. Instead, they're squeezed beneath my legs, on my feet, down the side of the bowl. They must be touching me.

When I watch TV, I have one dog draped about my neck, another in my lap, a third pressing my legs on the ottoman. They must touch me but seldom touch one another.

My wife Dee sleeps curled like a pretzel. Why? She loves her dogs and will deny them nothing. Matter of fact, she has a sign hanging over the kitchen stove that says:

LOST
HUSBAND, SHOTGUN, AND DOG
REWARD FOR DOG

On her refrigerator a magnet shows a man and woman in bed with a dog between their feet. The text says:

WE'RE STAYING TOGETHER
FOR THE SAKE OF THE DOG

When Dee sleeps, the dogs pin her with the blankets to the bed. She can't move. She can hardly breathe. It's evident that those Lhasas' ecstacy is directly proportional to how many square inches of her skin they are touching. But the dogs fuss if they touch one another accidentally. *The important thing in a dog's life is a human.*

What I'm saying in all this is that dogs are extremely tactile. Touch is a primary sensation in their lives. And when you consider that skin is a mammal's largest organ, you can assess the strength of this craving.

Therefore we must assess the dog's skin, which, like his nose, is a sensory receptor.

THE SKIN

To bond with a dog, you need primarily to rub his ears, his belly, and most important, his nose. Never pat. Pat, and a dog will wince, clench his jaws, brace his neck. It's too much like striking. But rub or massage, and the dog melts, leans into you, whimpers, and turns to mush. The amount of bonding is directly related to the amount of intimacy a master or mistress shares with his or her dog.

MASTER, MISTRESS, OR NEITHER?

Now let's get our terms straight. "Master" and "mistress" are archaic terms growing out of an age when animals were not considered property. That's what an 1880s New Mexico judge ruled when a British rancher named Montague Stevens filed charges against a man who stole one of his hounds. The court threw out the case, ruling, "A dog by legal statute is a wild animal, furthermore since no taxes was paid upon him, he was not regarded as property. Therefore, stealing a dog was not a crime."

But there was justice, of a sort. The judge ruled Stevens could "sue the culprit for inadvertently stealing the collar the dog wore."

So there was a time in America when a dog was worth less than the collar around his neck.

Anyway, the terms "master," "mistress," and "owner" are all out in this book. A person who has bonded with a dog is a human partner. And, some would say, a human parent.

Go to a vet, or groomer, and after a while, the receptionist will produce a puppy, saying, "Now here's your daddy. See? Everything will be all right."

Dee doesn't talk of her dogs, she talks of her kids.

More About Skin

If I told you to rub the dog's nose previously, that's not quite right. What you do is take the palm of your hand and place it over his nose, like a cup. Now the dog feels your skin, and he smells you—maximum stimulation. Dogs love this. Try it. Another thing that bonds them to you is to take your palms, bunch the dog's skin up from his cheeks, and cover his eyes, which you rub lightly. I've never known a dog who didn't melt for this. And best of all, get the dog on a high table or bed, love him, and blow your breath in his nose. This is ultimate bonding.

Now, before proceeding with the skin, let's make this point. Dogs who are permitted to intermingle, unneutered, and in defiance of leash laws, are permitted to run wild. Or dogs isolated out back and chained in snow or sun to a stake, who seldom see a human, never having a chance for contact—all these dogs will turn to one another.

But this pack behavior that canine behaviorists have spoken about for years is null and void for the bonded dog. The only pack for this dog is his human partners. And the dog will turn to another dog for fun or comfort only when his human partners are not around.

SHARED LIVES

That's because we now live with our dogs so they learn every nuance of our facial expressions, voice, posture, body odor, and so on. Their whole life becomes us; and, in many cases, they become our lives, too. Veterinarians talk about this, and I know they think about this, they even acknowledge this—but as you shall see in the last chapter, they don't have it all down pat. And they must.

Man is no longer a master, and his dog an animal subordinate. The two are now equals, and they are now lovers. Pure and simple. And if you doubt this, go to a local vet's office and stand in the reception room and watch the pathos. The 250-pound gray-haired man holding the pug hit by a car, convulsing until you feel he'll collapse with a stroke.

A lady learning that her dog just died runs to the clinic's door and falls to the floor, screaming until the staff carries her to an examining room.

A woman, upon learning it will cost three hundred dollars to repair her dog's mangled leg, tells the vet, "Put her to sleep." And the vet—who has a heart—takes the dog, repairs the leg, and adopts her out the back door. For this vet says, "To me there is no such thing as euthanasia. They're asking me to kill the dog. I'm here to heal . . . not kill."

DEATH ROW

Or go walk down death row in a governmental animal shelter. I was once on the board of a large-city animal agency. I'd sit there before the gray door to the "last mile," where we could hear the kennel man release the gate, and take a dog down the hall to his death. I had to quit. I couldn't stop the killing.

So I know what I'm talking about when I describe an old shepherd, the one with his feet upon the bars, his pleading eyes, the exposed tongue, the whimper, the trembling flanks, the wagging tail. Or that other dog, who presses his whole body flat into the door. Remember, skin—touch. This dog is getting as near to you with his skin as he can.

Now that old shepherd has only three seconds to display as you go by, so he pulls out all the stops and gives you every signal of love he can muster. For you're his ticket out: "Take me," he's saying, "and I'll love you."

So is this dog identifying with the dog next door who's pressing the gate? Or another sharing his kennel run? The people who believe the pack concept would say yes. The important thing to a dog is another dog, they would say. Crap. This dog's begging you, a human being, to become his mom or dad and get him the hell out of there. This dog is asking you to save his life.

And that's what all dogs ask. Cut off from their wildness and nature, they are helpless. If you are not prepared to play God, then never take on a dog. For you have the power of life or death over him. When he eats, where he sleeps, whether or not he gets a nutritionally balanced diet, whether or not you care enough to pay sixteen dollars for a parvo shot, whether or not you care enough to erect a wall so he can't barge into the street and be hit by a car. Only our parents ever cared this much for us: And that's what you must be for Pup! So if we want to treat our dogs as our babies, then all that means to me is we're humane, we have feelings, we acknowledge our responsibility to another living thing, and we're in love.

Then and Now

Gone are the days of animal neglect. My dad may have told me, "If the damned dog wants to eat, let him go find a rabbit." And when all my coax-home dogs either experienced distemper, scratched themselves silly from mange, or were hit by cars in the street, Mother would make me the only medicine she had, a bowl of white gravy, and I'd crawl under the house to see if the old dog would lap. Amazingly enough, that gravy saw many a pooch come crawling out of that dark recess and run and play another day.

But now our dogs have the best of diets and care. Just yesterday two of our Lhasas had ultrasound scans and another underwent a series of X rays. I took home a case of saline flushes for the old dog who's dying, and we bought a case of dog food. The bill? Two hundred and ninety dollars.

How do Dee and I pay for that? We drive old cars, we don't go to movies, we shop at Sam's Club, I wear clothes I've had thirty years (I've got neckties two inches wide), we forgo exotic dental procedures for ourselves.

For recreation we'll sometimes drive to the pharmacy and read the humorous greeting cards. Or we'll take the dogs and park in front of a pet store so they can bark at the mutts who walk by on leashes. And we do all this because our dogs are more vital and precious and exhilarating to us than a cruise, a trip to Branson, a country club, a pool out back, or a new pickup. And this book is written for several million Americans just like us, who'd cash in their IRAs if it meant Pup could live just one more year.

Back to This Nonsense about the Pack

Now this is not to say our house dogs do not have a social structure. There is a queen mother; there is a bitch who usurped her position; there is the recluse who's given up all hope of rank and status. There are two pups still digging holes, and the bonbon gal who is so above it all that she lies on the sofa and does her nails while she ignores the melee beneath her. And so on. But all this is irrelevant when Mom or Dad is around. Humans are the source of these dogs' lives, the source of the dog family's joy and shelter and sustenance and identity: They are the authority and the pillow.

ONCE MORE, THE SKIN

Okay, enough of that. Let's finish with the dog's skin. It's been theorized that a dog through his skin can predict an earthquake, feel static electricity, sense incoming storms. There are dogs who can predict their human partner's epileptic fits. Do they do that with their skin? I wonder.

For you see the skin has many receptor organs: Again we're talking about communication. The skin is a receiver. These receptors register cold, warmth, pressure, vibration, touch, and pain. Most important to us is this: These touch receptors are scattered liberally over the entire skin.

Now know this about your dog—about all dogs. They are extremely inefficient in ridding themselves of surplus heat. They just have so few sweat conductors, those being in the pads of the paws and the tongue. Working-dog trainers are aware of this, and it is a common truth that a dog can stand a ton of cold better than an ounce of heat.

Let me explain something unique about Dee and me right now. We've been away from our home in Sedona, Arizona, for three years seeking treatment for my advanced arthritis. To that end, we are presently seeing a doctor in Las Vegas, Nevada. We rented a place (Vegas is a boomtown and rentals are sky-high), and we live there on mixed stick furniture, some good stuff, and milk crates. Well, as I write this book, it's hot as hell here, and the dogs are miserable.

So last week I took them to Sedona, and what a change. It's cool there, and the dogs got "up," as we say, turning active, happy, vibrant, eager, loving, playful. If you've got a down dog, check his body heat.

HEAT

The dog's tummy is comparable to a human's wrist. That's where the largest supply of superficial blood vessels is closest to the skin. This is where you apply a coolant to lower the dog's body heat.

You can make a loving gesture by doing this during hot weather.

But more than that, you can save your dog's life. Pup's normal body temperature is 101.5 degrees Fahrenheit. Heatstroke can send this temperature soaring. When this happens, it causes tremendous congestion, which impedes circulation to the brain. This, in turn, creates pressure that can damage brain cells. So apply ice to the base of Pup's skull to cool him down.

Remember. The dog's skin is our primary way to give affection. We do this also with our voice, and with dispensed treats, and with just all-around good cheer. But to soothe a dog, to tell him you love him, to give yourself a therapeutic break, touch his skin.

THE EYE: ANOTHER SENSOR

The retina of the dog's eye is made up, in part, of rods and cones. Rods are sensitive to low intensities of light. Cones are also light sensitive, but they register color as well.

Dogs have more rods in relation to cones than humans do. Consequently, dogs can see better than we can at dusk and dawn. They also have a light-reflecting layer in the eye (the *tapetum lucidum)*, which intensifies vision of things we can barely see with the same amount of illumination. This layer, incidentally, is what causes those yellow eyes in a snapshot of your dog taken with a flash. First shine a light at the dog's eyes, then use your flash. There'll be no more of those yellow, glaring holes.

Another difference between the dog's eyes and ours is that his are more discriminating of movement and less of detail. If a dog is looking for you and you stand perfectly still, he can't make you out. (Ask any rabbit.) But move one inch, and he'll have you.

Dogs also have phenomenal peripheral vision. They can see sideways because dogs have 250 to 275 degrees of visual field and we have only 180. Dogs will catch any movement out of the corners of their eyes. But they pay for this by having very poor binocular vision. (However, trained working dogs can see their handlers up to a mile.) Neither do dogs see things up close very well. But dogs have never had a need for close-up sight. Their enemies and their meals-on-foot have appeared since the beginning of time some twelve yards before them.

A dog's eyes are a big factor in communicating with us, or in our interrelationship. Since they can see well in the dark they won't move when you get up at night. So beware. They'll think you can see them, they won't move, and you'll fall flat on your face.

To repeat: Dogs don't see well at long distance. So if you're far off, they can't recognize you very well. Yet they do register well on movement. So your gait identifies you more to a dog than your physical features do.

Dogs monitor our daily movements with their eyes. And they show emotion with them as well. We can all tell a look of love. Or hurt. Or shame. And the dog's eyes reveal all these things.

The dog's eyes, then, are important training tools. We monitor them constantly for feedback so we can sustain or adjust our communication.

There's little on earth as beautiful as a dog's eyes. The dog's eyes seem epitomized by that song that mentioned watermelon wine. They're mellow, deep, soft, and filled with feeling.

But remember this from our discussion of dogs' eyes: It matters far more what we read in them than what they see in us. The dog's eyes can become our most important training tool.

WHAT BIG EARS YOU HAVE

Dogs have phenomenal hearing. To hear the mailman walk down the sidewalk seems a miracle to me: Dogs can do it. To identify Dee's car a block before she enters the garage also seems miraculous.

Most humans have a hearing range of up to thirty thousand cycles. But dogs have an upper limit that reaches three times as high. In other words, dogs can hear ultrasonic sound. This is the way the wild dog locates a rodent or any other squeaking prey.

Incidentally, this is why women make the best puppy trainers.

They generally have high voices, which they effect when emulating baby talk. Pups love this. It excites and pleases them. They run to the woman and leap up for her and fall back, and the woman giggles and rubs the pup's belly. The pup knows he just died and went to heaven.

Same with children. No human can socialize a pup like a child. Or a bunch of kids. Roughhoused? Never mind. It doesn't hurt. The pup hears shrieks and sees creatures running around, and he must participate. Remember, dogs are athletes. More so than we will ever be. They want to run and heave hard, then stop out of breath and bound out again. They want to tumble and nip and scratch and scootch their jaws along the ground. And kids are rolling around down there, too. And they do it all together. Besides, kids are not six feet tall. They don't pose ominous figures like we adults do. They are the puppy's size.

Yes, if you've got yourself a houseful of kids you're going to have a mighty well-adjusted dog.

But remember this most about a dog's ears. They hear extremely well. I've whistled down Border collies a half-mile up a highland mountain. What I'm leading up to is that there's never a need to shout. Matter of fact, the greatest dog trainer of all time was Er Shelley of Columbus, Mississippi, and he actually whispered at his dogs. I'll tell you why later.

I was staggered the other day when I attended a dog-award ceremony at Ruston, Louisiana, where I met a man who had lost his voice to throat cancer. Bill Autrey of Alexandria, Louisiana, whispered to me in a grating voice that he trained up a Grand Hunting Retriever Champion out of his Labrador retriever Missy. (This is a herculean accomplishment, folks.) And the man couldn't speak above a whisper. And he handled his Lab to a grand championship that required the dog to work up to three hundred yards distant.

Remember this, then: Don't yell. Pup can hear you.

This girl and pup share secrets to last a lifetime. No one can bring up a pup like a child can.

THE EYES HAVE IT

A trait peculiar to most animals but highly developed in the dog is the ability to read our eyes: In other words, a dog is not all nose. Only the human partner who can read a dog's eyes will ever understand him, or control him.

Beryl Markham tells us of this with African lions. In her book, *West with the Night,* she recounts how she, in company with two Masai warriors, barged in on a lion covering a fresh kill.

The lion was mighty upset and let them know it. One Masai warrior told Beryl, "Observe his eyes, he thinks hard on many things." Later the Masai led Beryl past the feeding lion and she related, "I do not know how he knew that that particular instant was the right instant or how he knew that the lion would accept a truce."

I'll answer Beryl. It's called reading an animal. It's as imperative for dog training as it is for evading the attack of a feeding lion. And how do you teach something that's uniquely innate? That's barely explainable? Maybe something that's even God-given?

I don't know if you can. All I know is that I can stand before a pack of dogs and tell you what each of them is thinking. The man or woman beside me may not have a clue. So I start explaining. Some get it, some don't. It comes only after years of living intimately with animals. There's no shortcut for predicting animal behavior unless you've interpreted the clues, plus the behavior both preceding and following the clues, a thousand times. Or, said another way: You've conquered FIDO with a thousand pooches.

During seven years of legal duck seasons, I sat in a blind 420 straight days with essentially one dog. I learned to keep my head down, for the white flash of my face would flare the ducks. But I would look at this dog's eyes. Those eyes told me where the ducks were and what they were doing in every foot of flight. And he, and other dogs I took to the blind, could especially do this with peripheral vision. They would catch a duck coming in toward either of my shoulders, where I wouldn't see it until it flashed before me.

I would fire and harvest a duck for dinner, and the dog would not break; instead, he would turn and look into my eyes and the eyes would tell him if it was all right to go ahead and fetch the duck or wait because another duck might be coming in.

And I could tell by the dog's eyes if he were up for a hearty retrieve (I took many geriatric retrievers with me; you must learn that dogs love to work). For there may be skimmed ice on the pond, or the decoys might actually be frozen in the ice. Some mornings a dog would feel hearty, another morning not. I could read that. And I would either send him or keep him in the blind, depending on what his eyes told me.

Another example. Many times I've left my car and walked to the porch of a farmhouse to ask permission to hunt quail. Charging from around the corners of the house or from under the porch would be a swarm of displaying dogs. I would give them the eye and merely speak to see them disperse or go silly with too much display of wagging tails. Another man? He may try to reach that porch through the same milling pack and end up on a tree limb.

I read dogs' eyes, their hackles, the cock of their ears, the cascade of muscles over their shoulders, their posture and posing with one another, their laughing, their fright.

The Eyes are Pup's Way of Telling Us How He Feels

The human partner is Pup's first line of defense against illness and death. I was visiting a friend in Mississippi who had a rat terrier. I took one look at this man's dog and told him, "Your dog is sick." I read it in the eyes. The man challenged my diagnosis. I told him to believe me or not, but at least give the dog some medicine.

The man delayed taking the dog to a vet. It died within the month. When a dog is listless, his body pressed against the floor or sofa, head down, ears flat, and eyes without light—beware. You're probably looking at a sick dog.

I go to the vet and tell him, "My dog is sick."

The vet asks, "How do you know?"

I say, "She's down in the eyes."

The vet says, "What?"

"Down in the eyes," I repeat.

One vet after another will shake his head. But when the blood and urine samples come back he must concur—the dog is sick. I read it in the dog's eyes, and once you've bonded with your dog, you can, too.

WHAT DO DOGS SENSE?

Delmar Smith of Edmond, Oklahoma, may be the world's top gun-dog trainer. Delmar just has a way with animals. At nine years of age, he was training horses after school and earning a man's wages. He later trained dogs to win ten national Brittany championships.

So a bunch of chalk-eyed cowboys were draped on the corral poles at Delmar's, and ol' Delmar was always buying "ruined" pleasure horses and putting a mouth back on them and selling them for a pretty penny.

Delmar Smith is America's seminar dog trainer. He'll soon be in your town.

You see, a person who doesn't know anything about a horse will ride the bit so much that the horse will desensitize and become a runaway. He'll no longer respond to bit commands. But Delmar will resensitize these horses' mouths and make them valuable again.

Anyway, out of the horse trailer came this would-be mustang, just raring up and cleaving the air with his front hooves and frothing at the mouth and looking bug-eyed. Delmar slid through the poles and walked up to the horse. He said something to him. And the horse came down and quit his displaying and Delmar touched his cheek, turned away, and the horse followed like he wanted to put his nose in Delmar's pocket.

That's the gift.

Ain't many who have it.

So what did we witness? We witnessed a communication of feeling—or scent.

Or consider the unique gift of Hoyle Eaton, Booneville, Missis-

Hall-of-fame dog trainer Hoyle Eaton shows off his prize pup.

sippi. Hoyle has won the National Bird Dog Championship four times and is a member of the Field Trial Hall of Fame.

Hoyle and his wife were returning from some dog-award banquet when they stopped for gas. Hoyle tells us, "This attendant was standing here and there was a counter there, and there was a candy bar behind the counter I wanted. So I started to step back there and get it, and the attendant shouted, 'Don't go back there. That dog will eat you up.' Now, I didn't know there was a dog back there. So I took the guy at his word.

"I walked outside and sat down in a chair. I picked up a paper and was reading it while he was getting the car ready. And I wasn't paying any attention. In a little bit a dog came up and put his head on my leg. And I didn't think who the dog was. I was just petting him and reading the paper. And the man got through with the car and come back and saw that guard dog and me and he couldn't believe it. He was incredulous. And he asked me, 'What do you do?' And I told him I train dogs. He just shook his head. And I hadn't said a word to that dog."

Hoyle explains, "You have to know what dogs are saying: They are always telling you something. I can pretty well tell by their expressions and by their body movements. I go by that a lot. The way they present themselves to me."

We accept what Hoyle says, for we've learned this truth by now. But there's something else that occurred here. The guard dog was also reading Hoyle.

So what did we witness? A communication of words? No, a communication of feelings. FIDO!

THE GIFT

It's my hope that when you finish this book, you can do a little reading of dogs on your own—and they can read you. But first, there's more to a dog than his skin and nose and eyes and tail. What else must we consider? Let's see.

Words ain't the whole of it, nor scent, nor ESP, nor body language, nor touch, nor sound, nor whatever God's gift might be. I've known so many of these men who have the gift. The one trait they share is a genuine friendship with everyone they meet and a soft and cordial way about them that makes you relax. I've seen it with dogs around these men. The dogs lose their tenseness, their fright, their uncertainty. And it happens in one second. Maybe that's what we must all learn to do. Relax.

That's quite a challenge for today's harried Americans, ain't it?

6

Who Do You Know Like This?

I know a couple whose old dog died, and they buried her in the backyard. When they had to move, they dug the dog up and took her with them. Dogs mean more to us now than ever before. If you don't understand this, then you don't know the extent of modern man's need for selfless love.

The bond you have with your dog exists outside twenty-first-century man's everyday greed, self-centeredness, chicanery, and suspicion.

At last there's something you can love that won't hurt you.

The dog is constant. He'll not betray you, leave you, or diminish his love for you. He's the most exact and constant emotional partner the world has ever known—and he always will be.

For one thing, dogs don't judge. Do you know how miraculous this is?

Some homeless ragtag who sleeps under the interstate overpass picks up a pup, and the pup bonds for life. No questions asked. He doesn't bother you, or other dogs, by asking, "Could I have done better with someone else?"

Or that same dog can be adopted by the president of the American Kennel Club who lives on a Long Island estate, and the dog will never know the difference, and he will never care.

Read that line again. He will never know the difference, and he will never care. The import of this realization is staggering.

WHO DO YOU KNOW LIKE THIS?

We have all read in the newspaper about a woman who died and left $14 million to her 150 dogs.

"That's stupid," the disgruntled said. "Lots of people could have put that money to good use." And likely among that group of worthy recipients would be themselves.

But I ask the critics of this woman's will to consider this:

Remember that time you came by a pup? All the doubts. Puddles on the carpet. Gnawed shoelaces. Milk drips on the kitchen floor. But for reasons of your own, the pup moved in.

And how did he come through the door?

Did he say, "Hi," so you could understand? Was he fluent in English? Did he come bearing gifts? Did he represent a social coup? Had he done things? Been places? No?

Well, then, if he didn't have any of these things going for him, then surely he was pedigreed. They're worth money, you know. Oh, you say you gave a kid who had a box of pups in front of the grocery store two dollars for him. Well, was he pretty to look at, then? "No, kind of rangy," you say, "and wobble-kneed and pinched-nosed." Well, then, was he strong or fearless? Could he do some work, help protect the place? What's that? How strong and fearless can a pup be at seven weeks? I see your point.

Then let's face it. That pup came into your home absolutely worthless and a total foreigner. I ask you, how many of those types have you taken in lately?

And when this improbable guest got through the door, what did he do? I see. He puddled on the carpet, gnawed shoestrings, dripped milk.

So you threw him out, right?

Nope, wrong.

Why was this?

Well, when that pup came through the door, he had three things going for him: a wagging tail, a rough, wet tongue, and an eagerness to say hello to everyone in sight.

It was as if meeting you made his day. He quivered with excitement. Rolled over in submission. Nuzzled up so the warmth of his body came soothing to your heart through the skin of your ankle. So you picked him up. That's the way with love. It's contagious.

And you stood there holding this pup close to your cheek smelling that last-night's-ice-cream-carton smell of him, your fingers sunken into his soft belly, woven through his silky hair, when across your face goes that rough, wet tongue. What you had in your hands was absolute, nondiluted, ever-growing, nondemanding, never-judging, I-can't-live-without-you, take-me-wherever-you-go, hurry-back-if-you've-got-to-leave love.

And I ask you this question:

Who do you have in mind, like this, to leave your money to?

Be Careful What You Teach the Dog and Don't Know You're Doing It

One of the most fascinating aspects of dogs I ever discovered is how stimulus-bound they can become. When Dee met me, I had twenty-nine working dogs of my own and one house schnauzer. The big dogs were Labrador retrievers, Australian shepherds, Border collies, English and Irish setters, Welsh springer spaniels, and one 160-pound Great Pyrenees named Moby who patrolled the farmyard. There was also a mom-and-dad coyote team named Bonnie and Clyde. I kept the coyotes for training, in hopes I could find some bridge between wild and tame dogs that had not been noticed before. I also wanted to see how far I could go with heel, sit, and stay using wild dogs, in hopes of better training their domestic cousins.

This gal's T-shirt tells the world, "The more I know men the better I like my dog." Sorry, guys.

Each year I'd raise a litter of coyotes and experiment with them. The coyotes were kept in a twenty-four-foot-long by four-foot-wide kennel run.

To whatever degree I'd win or fail with training the coyote pups, I'd release them at about twelve weeks of age to make their way in the world. And this is where I was stunned.

All these coyote pups' lives—being twelve weeks—was spent in a linear world twenty-four feet long. They'd pace back and forth most every waking moment of their puppy lives.

When the gate was sprung, I watched the six of them hurl themselves down the hill toward the creek in front of the kennel. They made a beeline. No veering. Not even thinking of it. They did not try to skirt the creek—there was a footbridge close by—but splashed pell-mell into it. Then up, in a straight line, on the far hill.

Days went by. Then one afternoon I was driving to town when my car kicked up a coyote in a roadside ditch. It was one of my pups. The pup began running along the side of the road (in his mind he was back in his twenty-four-foot-long kennel run). He ran and ran in a straight line with no thought and seemingly no capability to veer left or right. But a half-mile away he hit an intersecting railroad track—another straight line—and abruptly turned to the side. And I watched him bore into the unknown down those silver rails. Now the railroad tracks were his old kennel run.

And it hit me, and I sat there—I never attempted to teach it, never thought of it, never dreamed of it. But I had raised a litter of coyotes that could run only in a straight line—in no matter how perilous a plight they found themselves.

ONE-WAY COYOTE

They were stimulus-bound.

That concept comes from psychology. Give a chimpanzee a hammer to hit a peg with and reward him with a tidbit. But what happens? The chimpanzee uses the hammer for jobs the tool was never intended—and on which it never works. Why? Because the chimp is stimulus-bound.

And sitting beside the railroad tracks I then knew: *Everything that happens to a pup in his first days conditions him for life.* Conditions? Yes, predisposes him to be one way. Like a sculptor conditions (sets with his hands) some beeswax in the form of a horse. The beeswax is later converted to bronze, and the bronze will never be anything else—a horse it will be forevermore.

And so it was with the coyotes. Forevermore they will run in a straight line when their capability, if reared in the wild, would have been that of a broken-field runner, zigzagging everywhere, doubling back, leaping to the side, feinting.

I had tampered with nature and made a one-way coyote.

So what this means to us, and for us, is that everything we do with a pup in his early life will affect him as long as he lives.

So we must be very, very careful.

The House Pack

When you have a large family of dogs in your house, you must be a tactician. Candy is fed by the back door, Sugar in front of the sofa, Chili behind the big chair, Muffy in front of the sink. But what of the new twins, Puddin and Tiff?

Well, they've got to be isolated. If not, they will run to every dog's plate to see what's in it. So the twins are put in the utility room with an expandable portable gate (every dog owner must have one of these). And the weeks pass by.

But the twins don't want to go back there anymore. They want to be treated like the big dogs. So I try it, but it doesn't work. They create havoc trying to steal from every dog's plate.

So what to do?

All right, I take the portable gate and move it to cover the door into the living room. Now I've tripled the space the twins have. They can eat in the utility room, but can also come down the hallway and see what every other dog is doing.

So what happens?

The twins never appear.

Just having been put in the utility room—without a gate—they fence their own selves in. That's right, I go to look and they're sitting before the washer and dryer—with no gate holding them there—waiting for me to come let them through a gate that no longer exists.

So remember. *Each thing we do with a pup is teaching him something.* Don't forget this. It will make us or break us as trainers.

And how about the newspaperman in Scott City, Kansas, where the annual cycle is summer wheat and winter snow. Well, Buck, a nine-year-old Labrador retriever, now delivers his human partner's paper to each subscriber. The dog takes the paper on the command "fetch," leaps out of the truck, lays the paper on the porch, and jumps back into the cab's warmth to await the next household.

I'll bet you Buck knows the route by memory, just from accompanying his human partner morning after morning as he makes his rounds.

SOME DOGS ARE VERY BRIGHT

And what of very bright dogs like Candy? It was Dee's birthday, and of course all her birthday cards have dogs on them. So one of the cards was propped in a window, and suddenly Candy saw it and raised up, her paws on the wall, and barked at the picture. Candy knows a dog even if it's made of cardboard and stands only four inches tall.

So what do you want to teach—or, more amazingly, have a dog learn? Well, let's go get a pup so we can get started. So we can see the miracle unfold.

Part Two

Bonding with Pup

7

If You Were a Pup, Would You Pick You?

Pups are taught with feeling, not words. They respond to gestures, body language, facial expressions, tone of voice, body odors, and what they feel: FIDO! They must have a trainer who is patient, considerate, bright, loving, needing, wanting, and sensitive enough to know what a dog's asking for when he apparently needs nothing. If you can't be these things, then let Pup go. It ain't the picker that's important to me: it's the pup who's picked and the kind of life the picker can assure him.

Certain human types want (or need) certain dog types. Children should have a cocker spaniel, English springer spaniel, English setter, golden retriever, Brittany spaniel—to name a few.

What we're looking for is a naturally happy dog, a mellow dog, a midsize dog. A dog with so much bottom in him that he'll endure the harassment of a child, the tugging and pulling. The dressing him up in old clothes and forcing him into the plastic wading pool or playing in the sandpile.

For the past twenty-three years, I've been gun-dog editor for *Field & Stream* magazine. During that time, I've interviewed thousands of dog owners. And each time I ask them why they chose their breed of dog, they always tell me, "Because of its temperament." Not its bird-finding ability, not its imperviousness to cold water, not its nose, not its running gear—all of which would be important in a hunting dog—but instead because the dog is good around the house and gentle with the children.

So the grizzled old gun dog with the drive to broach multiflora rose hedges and work all day in belly-scraping stubble and hunt amid cacti—receives his ultimate test before the hearth, not before the bird.

THE WORK DOG

Functional people need a functional dog. Labrador retrievers are the pick for service dogs, fire dogs, bomb dogs, drug-detection dogs, waterfowl and upland-game dogs, guide dogs for the blind and the

I was fishing on the Mississippi south of New Orleans when this oyster boat passed by. The yellow Lab lives his life aboard this boat. Nowadays, we can find dogs everywhere at work—some of our nation's congressmen take dogs to their offices on Capitol Hill.

deaf, avalanche dogs, and water-rescue dogs. There's mighty little you can't teach a Labrador retriever.

Other work dogs are German shepherds, any other shepherd, golden retrievers, and some spaniels.

These dogs make superlative house pets. However, they are seldom good watchdogs; and, except for the police dog, never attack dogs. They are just too mellow.

The Farm Dog

Farmers and ranchers need Australian shepherds, border collies, collies, Corgis, kelpies, old English sheepdogs, German shepherds, Shetland sheepdogs, Belgian sheepdogs, and on and on.

Incidentally, I've found border collies to be the smartest of all dogs. There's nothing they can't do. Take Temple Henderson of Hunt, Texas. Temple farms. There he was on his tractor one day,

I love border collies; they've got all the smarts.

plowing in ever-smaller circles, when his border collie began chasing a rabbit. Temple shouted to him, "Bring that rabbit here."

The dog ran the rabbit in ever-tightening circles until finally, with the rabbit exhausted, the collie herded him directly under the tractor, where Temple reached down and picked the rabbit up by its ears.

Yes, a border collie can do anything, and he understands every word you say to him. Some of my most pleasant days were spent working sheep in the Scottish Highlands with border collies.

THE LOVE DOG

Older people need a dog who won't jerk their arms out of their sockets, something small enough to pick up and handle with arthritic hands, an entertaining and seldom depressed critter.

Such dogs include poodles, Lhasa apsos, Shih Tzus, Pomeranians, toy fox terriers, toy Manchester terriers, West Highland white terriers, Scottish terriers, chihuahuas, rat terriers, Norfolk and Norwich terriers, Pekingeses, Tibetan spaniels, Tibetan terriers, and pugs. To name a few.

THE SPORTSMAN'S DOG

The hunter wants a vizsla, Weimaraner, pudelpointer, wire haired pointing griffon, Labrador retriever, golden retriever, flat-coated retriever, Chesapeake Bay retriever, American water spaniel, English setter, English pointer, Brittany spaniel, German shorthaired pointer, German wirehaired pointer, and on and on.

THE DETERRENT DOGS

Machos, those contemporary dudes with Mohawk hairdos and tattoos on the backs of their shoulders, plus some gals from fifteen to thirty-five, want a Great Pyrenees, puli, German shepherd, doberman pinscher, Great Dane, rottweiler, English bulldog, boxer, or anything that looks like it could devour its metal water bucket.

I wouldn't have such a large dog around because I don't want to scoop up a mess that big anymore. And did you ever consider how you're going to lift one of those guys if he goes lame, or is too sick to walk from your car to the clinic? With my arthritis, I couldn't help him. So I'll leave the giants to guys and gals better suited to handle a hundred pounds of deadweight.

The Cur

And so it goes, and so it should. But there's one dog we've overlooked and that may be the best of all: the common mongrel. Why? For so many reasons, but I'll cite you two: They are generally more hardy because they have crossbred vigor, and they are less inclined to genetic deficiencies. I've often found mongrels to be brighter, tougher, happier, and more self-sufficient than the blooded variety. Don't ever overlook the pup whose mother never married.

It's interesting to reflect that after a career of helping millions train their dogs I recall the best gun dog I ever went to field with was one-quarter German shorthaired pointer, and three-quarters English pointer: i.e., a cur. Even a nonhunter will enjoy reading about Ol' George, as he was called, in the book *Pick of the Litter*, published by the publisher of this book.

Our Dogs

Our dog Muffy is the daughter of a Lhasa apso and a free spirit who found a hole in the fence. She is a jewel. Her sense of duty is unfathomable. Now she is dying, but this morning she managed to get out of the house and onto the grass before she vomited. She did this with pancreatitis, a calcium-blocked kidney, Cushing's disease, a liver ruined by the wrong medicine, and a repaired herniated disk that hinders her locomotion. How many people would have been so committed under these physical limitations? God, I love her sense of duty and responsibility. God, I love dogs.

Candy is a Lhasa-Maltese mix with a huge motor in her, a brain as adept as an IBM computer, and a personality that could help a barker sell a wagonload of elixir to a crowd of Christian Scientists.

The twins, Tiffany and Puddin, are the offspring of a Lhasa and a bichon frise. Their unique talent is unrelenting love.

The only Lhasa bluebloods we have are Chili, who is a recluse, and Sugar, who is my nurse. One time, when I was bedridden, Sugar never left my right shoulder. Sugar's fortes are compassion and conscientiousness. When all the other dogs bark, which is a no-no (for I'm respectful of my neighbors' peace and quiet) Sugar comes directly to me, as if to say, "It's not me, Dad." She is my dog, bonded tighter than Super Glue. And she'd accompany me anywhere, except that she upchucks in the car.

Chili is the hole and tunnel finder. You never see Chili except at lunchtime. Not only does Chili reject Dee and me, but she also rejects the other dogs. Chili truly wants to be left alone. To her we're all a bunch of riffraff.

SEX

All our dogs are female, spayed, and under twenty pounds.

And you'll probably wonder: Why females? Well, sex is a distraction. Females are rendered strange by it twice a year. But it's never off the mind of a male. When you get the female spayed, she's normal the whole year round. Any negative consequence of spaying or neutering? Just that the dog will gain weight if you don't monitor its diet.

Females are docile, yielding, loving, desirous of pleasing, and less concerned with social ranking than males. (Oh, yes, I know. In the wild, the pack is usually headed up by an old bitch. But in a house, where the gals have bonded with Mom and Dad, that canine adjust-

Sugar's the looker in the family.

Like something wild emerging from a hole, Chili sneers to drive us all away.

ing among themselves becomes moot.) And if you say that's because I've repressed them, beat them down, aha!

Males of all species can be bullies, strong-willed, with heavy-duty strength, deep loyalties, scrappiness, a love to work, a strong independence, plus a reluctance to forgo the challenge of seeing who's going to run the place. Besides, as puppies, they can be chronic biters, whereas females are more likely to gum your fingers since what they crave is love.

A good example: When you are digging a hole in the yard to plant a flower, a female pup will sit there, lick your hand, and sniff the hole. The male pup will shove your hand out of the way and dig the hole to suit himself.

LHASA APSOS

And I can hear you ask: Why Lhasas? Lhasas are gritty, tenacious, athletic, quick-witted, one-partner dogs, who specialize in cuddling. But they take no crap from anybody. Get heavy-handed with them, and they'll bite you. Yell and they'll turn you off. Threaten and they'll walk away with more nonchalant hip motion than a Las Vegas chorus girl. Yes, Lhasas are rugged as a Harley, snippy as a Metro dweller, and cute as a cheerleader.

But alas, some Lhasas make poor children's dogs. If kids hit them, the Lhasa may bite back. Many Lhasas have a volatile temper and won't think twice about leaving their teeth prints in your ankle. A good name for a male Lhasa would be "Ballistic."

Since Lhasas are inbred sentinel dogs, they have one oddity in their makeup. Have anyone appear in the yard or move anything in the house, and they'll alert on it, barking until nightfall. Move a vase on a bureau, the rascals will notice it. They want their world left just like it is. I've never known another breed—or human—to be so observant, or to seek such permanency. Dee and I moved from one house to another. Such upheaval actually made the Lhasas sick. They can't stand uncertainty or disarray.

THE SCRAPPER

One day Candy and I walked into the garage where a plumber working upstairs had left his rottweiler. Candy attacked. The rottweiler stood with Candy in a death grip—hanging on the behemoth's lip a foot above the concrete floor. That's a Lhasa.

Another feature of the Lhasa that endears me is its small and compact size. Lhasas fit perfectly in the crook of your arm. And they are just the right size to ride on your left knee when you are driving into town.

Also—we might as well say this now—Lhasas think. Yes, dogs think. Some nights I pile the dogs in the car and take them for a ride. One night when we came home, there was Dee's car in the garage. So what? Well, Dee's territory is the Southwest, and she'd been gone two weeks on this trip. So I pulled into the garage, and immediately Candy started whining and scratching the window and, in general, just raising hell. Why? Seeing Dee's car, she knew her mommy was home, and she wanted out. Does Candy have the capability to think? All dogs think.

And finally, Lhasas were bred by the Buddhist lamas of Tibet to warn them of intruders. When a stranger shows up (and this could be a two-year-old child on a tricycle), a Lhasa goes berserk and barks until you are near deaf. Better live far off the road.

In conclusion, there's something about a Lhasa that makes me regard them as my grandchildren. I'm tipping my age, but I'm also applauding their unique charm . . . and their innate value.

No Two Alike

So I've listed certain breeds predisposed to certain human types. But, did you know there's often more difference in personality and character within a litter than between two breeds? And repeatedly I've seen more difference in dogs of the same species than when compared with other species.

That's the fascination of dogs. And that's why you always need about twenty. Because every dog is different, and watching its unique character emerge is a delight. You never know what you're going to get.

I raised Labrador retrievers for years; sold them at the farm. I saw people come and drag sticks, offer tidbits in a far corner of the kennel, take the pups to see if they'd hazard tall grass. And on and on.

Me? I'd rather spend my time praying than picking. Only God knows how each individual pup is going to turn out. You can give a pit bull to a wheelchair grandmother—the dog could be that timid and gentle and subdued. Or you could have a poodle who would disarm Mack the Knife.

Fanciers say each breed has a tendency, and to a point that's right. A pointer generally points, a retriever retrieves, and a flusher flushes. Also, a shepherd will herd and an Alsatian will keep you from crossing a barrier. But then all pronouncements must cease. Dogs are unique as fingerprints and don't ever forget it. Rather, revel in it. You'll have a ball.

For a while I raised Peke-a-poos, a delightful cur breed. While training Labs one day in a tall-grass field, Muffy (yes, I've used the name for several dogs) was watching from the kennel truck window. I had one Lab after another who couldn't find the dummy I had thrown. Finally, going to the truck and putting all the Labs away, I opened the door to get a drink of water and Muffy leaped out, tunneled through the tall grass, flipped up the dummy, and dragged it back to me, as if to say, "Here's the damned thing . . . now let's go home."

I was helping a neighbor train his Lab. He and his wife and the dog, plus Dee, myself, and a pair of twin westies we had fifteen years, were walking a rural golf course on a Sunday afternoon. The man picked up a stick and threw it in a pond. The Lab would not enter the water. The man threw another stick, then another.

Finally Punk, the female westie, waddled forward, slithered in, and pumped her way to the sticks. She grabbed one, turned about with a flip of her stub tail, stroked back, emerged on the bank, shook water, dropped the stick, and told me, "That's a stupid game."

The neighbor quit training his Lab.

A Working Championship

Breed books give you a standard: eighteen inches at the shoulders, eighteen to twenty-four pounds. Stuff like that. Bosh.

Dogs are not gauged that way. Those are show dogs, Hollywood types. And repeatedly, the show-dog breeders can create a degenerate lot when they mess with performance dogs.

Let me prove it.

When I was a lad, the cocker spaniel was the most popular dog in America. They had it all: spunk, endurance, love, cheerfulness, health—and they could get you a bird. Did you know they were named for the woodcock, which was their specialty in the hunting field?

Then the show people got hold of them. They stretched the cocker's ears so long, they now form an escalator for debris to leave the field and wind up in the ear cavity. Nowadays cockers have all sorts of ear problems. In other words, the original no-problem ear, bred up by sportsmen for a century, was foregone for beauty by the bench fancier. Only now are we getting the functional cocker back—by going to England for new blood.

Any feathered dog is in danger of being destroyed by the show set. Take the golden retriever, once regarded as the greatest of all upland game retrievers. Well, the golden had that beautiful copper fur. So they bred the dog to have even more fur. Until now, if the dog leaps into the pond for a duck, he could just about drown from the weight of water in his coat. And one more thing: Someone decided the dog would look better white. Yes, white. So now we have all these ghost-like goldens. Hmmmmm.

Same thing happened to the Irish setter. The show fanciers went for the long hair to the extent that the Irish setter is now a mobile dust mop. And on and on.

I'm going to tell you something. If you go look for a working pup and the breeder tells you that the pups he's offering are out of show champions, don't even reach for your coat, just get the hell out of there.

But let me say two things quick: If you want a show dog or want to be a sideline fan, then by all means pick a champion-bred pup. Those dogs are bona fide canines and have all the magnificent attributes of any dog.

But there is this. If those dogs up close in the pedigree show a working-dog championship, then get mighty interested in buying one of their pups. Look for CD, Companion Dog; CDX, Companion Dog Excellent; HRC, Hunting Retriever Champion; FTC, Field Trial Champion; UD, Utility Dog; UDT, Utility Dog Tracker; and ask about any other initials you see on the paper. You want one of these dogs for they've proven they have the biddability to accept training and the functional conformation to physically get the job done, and the temperament and smartness to make their lessons easy.

For you must know this. Dogs that compete in working champi-

"Really dah-ling, I can't give my autograph right now." That's show business!

onships are trained in a structured, formal, and demanding setting. They are asked to do so very much, and only the great ones make it. You'll always want one of their pups. There is one exception: retrievers who have field-trial championships. These dogs are asked to do such horrid things at field trials that they must trip over their God-given instincts. Unable to do so readily, they are too often electrically shocked to perform. That's right, shocked. Pups from such dogs have little more excellence in their makeup than the ability to take a high-voltage, low-amperage charge, and that's hardly what you want before your fireplace.

So get a dog that can get you out of a jam, can stand the long haul, can pitch in and help you out. Beauty's fine, but it never changed the tire in the rain on a remote road.

FUNCTIONAL CONFORMATION

So what is this thing called functional conformation? Let's consider the working dog.

A gun dog needs a big bone balcony over the eyes to knock stubble away, tight testicles to keep them from chafing after hunting all day in a cut milo field. These dogs require a large heart girth so that when they heat up, the rib cage expands, the lungs can enlarge, and the dog won't collapse from heatstroke. Same goes for the heart. It must be able to pump hard.

Eyelids must be dark for working in the sun. If they are light, they could be susceptible to skin cancer. Get those tails high, for that lengthens the pelvic drive muscles and gives a greater stroke of the wheel: i.e., the dog can run faster and farther.

The foot must be tight so it doesn't splat on impact. Splat and the dog can't get out of his crate the next morning.

And so it goes, on and on and on. In my gun-dog books, this list requires a full chapter.

So these are the things you want to look for in any dog. Things to help him enjoy his days, get around, be capable, do something.

Things that see him to old age, that keep him out of the vet's clinic, that give you those extra years of joy. One little fact: Terriers have the greatest longevity of any group of dogs. Want a companion for fifteen years? Get a terrier.

There are so many things important in conformation. Even something minor, like the way the teeth match. If they don't, we call it "overshot" and "undershot." Why would this concern us? Well, if the teeth don't match, then the bitch can disembowel the pup when she's trying to bite off the umbilical cord. That was one thing wrong with the Peke-a-poos. I'd have to sit there during birth and take each pup and cut the cord. These smashed-face dogs are just great candidates for unmatched jaws. But how I love those sassy faces!

So what I'm saying is this: No matter what breed of dog you choose, make sure you get one out of sturdy parents. There's as much difference within breeds as between breeds. Make sure you get a dog who can hold up over the long haul.

One Final Word

Now I want to disclose something about our dog family. None of these Lhasas has been trained formally.

This is important to disclose. Because critics will charge that I've so dominated these Lhasas and repressed them and controlled them that they've given up being dogs.

I've been training dogs all my adult life. And as a dog columnist, I'm exposed to over fourteen million readers each month. In other words, I've been a part of training a ton of dogs all over the world.

But I finally said, "I've had enough training for my personal dogs." I further said, "I'm content to let them self-train, for I've done all the nuts and bolts stuff and all the exotic stuff I ever intend to do. I now want to enjoy the rest of my life with some dogs that feel the same way I do."

So I decided I was going to raise a houseful of dogs who never heard the words "heel," "sit," "stay." And you know what?

They all turned out to be the best dog family I've ever been around. They've never had a collar on them, nor a lead—except to walk around the block or get from the car to the vet. All they've ever been asked to do was "come here," and yes, because they are hyper Lhasas, "knock off the noise."

So we're going to train dogs later, and I'll show you how to teach heel, sit, stay, and all that stuff. But you really don't need any of that for the best dog family the world has ever seen. These dogs know what you want. More than that, they want to give it. Train or not, the dog in your house will one day give you all you want—the same as if you'd formally trained him.

All you've got to do is show them facial expressions of approval or disappointment, and they'll self-train. Honest.

Don't ever lift a heavy hand. Don't ever lose your patience and lock the dog in a bathroom all day. Don't kick at one if he dives for a scrap under the table. Just be kind, enjoy this blessing, take it easy, relax, and let your blood pressure go down. (Incidentally, did you know when you touch a dog, his body functions also slow down—as well as your own?)

And I want to say one more thing before we continue. To tell the dog's story I must include my own. When I mention myself in this book it's not to put any spotlight on me. Everything I'm ever going to be I've already been. So the only reason I write is to help the 54 million dogs now living in 34 million American homes. And if mentioning something about Dee or me, or something about our dogs, helps get that done, then you're going to read about it.

Incidentally, the average dog owner is married, lives in a house as opposed to an apartment, condo, or town house, is under fifty years of age, and has no children living at home.

OVER THE BOUNDING MAIN

Right now I'll give one insight into what my dogs and I are like. When I had those twenty-nine working dogs, I sent off eighty-eight

Here's a dog out of my old world when I was training for the big field-trial circuit. This guy made many a swim behind the sailboat.

dollars and the end flap off a carton of Kools for a ten-foot Styrofoam Sunflower sailboat. When the radio announced a tornado warning (remember we lived in Kansas), I'd flip the latches on the kennel gates, launch that Sunflower, and we'd all take off.

Once the wind sucked me up, spun me around, flipped me upside down, and spiked the mast and me in the mud. Well, the mast was made of aluminum and broke, so I went to town and had one made of steel; and those twenty-nine dogs and I rode those happy waves again and again.

Now what I want to emphasize is this. *The dogs loved it.* Remember I told you the African (or Cape) hunting dogs simultaneously sensed encroachment or danger. Well, my dogs caught the fury of me, responded to my adrenaline, and attacked that outrageous water and wind with zest and glee.

I can see them now—leaping straight up in the water to get ahead of the pack, biting at the water in play, leaping on top of each other to give a dunking like a kid in a municipal pool.

And when that wind spiked me, you should have seen their concern. They dove for me, they clutched at me, they pushed on me—what else is there like a dog?

Many of those same dogs backpacked the Rockies with me; they carried their own food and learned to like trout.

And we put up birdhouses together, trimmed the fruit orchard, gathered the winter firewood, and slid, grunted, and fell together moving snow from the back door.

My point is: Do things with your dogs. They love it. And you will, too.

So having gotten this pep talk out of the way, don't you think it's time we went and got you a pup?

8

How About a Snotty Nose?

I walk among the dilapidated crates with screen floors to shed the droppings. I stop before each brood matron, look into her blank eyes, look at her stretched teats, her matted coat, her caked bottom, her stained paws. No one comes to coo to these dogs, to tell them they love them. Oh, someone comes in the morning to feed and clean up. Then maybe in the evening. But did these brood matron's paws ever touch dirt? Did they ever feel a loving hand? Have they ever run in the sunshine, or waded into a pond, leaped for a butterfly, or heard a child's laugh? Have they ever known a blanket, or the warmth of a stove, or just one time had a special treat? Well, they are puppy machines and their offspring are shipped all over the nation —you see them in the cages at the shopping center. Are these the mothers you want for your pups?

It ain't the pup you pick I care about, it's the guy or gal who does the picking. Many wonder: Is this pup good enough for me? While I'm wondering: Is this guy good enough for this pup?

I can't tell you what breed to pick, nor what price to pay, but I can tell you once you've gone shopping, which litter to pass up or which pup to take out of the litter that you finally find acceptable. For here's an expert to help me. You'll be mighty glad you listened to what he has to say.

DR. DICK ROYSE

He's sitting there, reared back, smoking his pipe. He has that bright, scrubbed, compact, orderly look of eggs in a crate. I've known Doc for thirty-five years. He was raised on a farm, joined the Navy, and came home to scoop kennels for a kind vet who convinced him to go to college. He is Dr. Dick Royse of Wichita, Kansas.

Never once in our thirty-five-year association was Doc too busy to answer my question. I'd stand beside him at surgery, and as he saved the dog, he filled me in. Didn't matter who the client was. If I phoned, he took the call. Through my reporting, Doc has now talked to 145 million dog readers over and over for twenty-two years. I cannot assess how much help he has done for the dog. Now he joins me at the farm on a Saturday afternoon and we sit in the kitchen as he says, "Bill, too many people are picking pups for the wrong reasons." He sucks on his pipe contemplatively. The pipe helps him think.

"They come into my clinic because they've gone to look for a pup and they've been taken in by this sad, waif-looking little thing that's either the runt, or undernourished, or has some type of impairment, or was sitting off in the corner of the pen all by himself, and appeared lonely. And Bill, it's a pitiful sight.

"So, out of compassion—and young people between eighteen and twenty-eight seem most susceptible to this, as though that lonely cast-off pup reflects something in their own lives—and feeling sorry for the pup, they take him home. And Bill . . . what you see is what you get."

Doc's left hand polishes the pipe bowl. His words ease out between the thin wisps of white smoke. "It's nice people are so compassionate. No quarrel with that. But it's unfortunate because of the end result. People must be more objective when picking a pup.

Compassion can just get them a very sick pup and a lot of problems and the grief that comes when the pup dies."

The Looks of the Place

"When a person goes to buy a pup," Doc says, "the first thing he should look for is cleanliness. Is the place clean, tidy, well-kept, bright-looking, happy-looking, free of flies and debris and broken-down pens? Does it smell to high heaven? Are ten pups crowded into one crate? It's difficult to get a healthy pup from ill-kept places.

"Then look at the pups. First, look at them in the litter. Which ones appear stronger, more active, more dominant? Which ones strut, up on their toes, perky-eared, bright-eyed? Which ones hold their ground? Which ones try to take the ground from you?

"When you've picked one who appeals to you, get him off by himself. Now what's his response? Is he still active, still eager, still peppy?"

(What Doc's looking for is a dog with a big motor in him and a lot of bottom, you know, like my Candy, she won't bottom out.)

"Granted, different people want different things in a dog. The go-getter wants a dog who'll go get 'em. I guess a junkyard man wants a junkyard dog. Such people seek traits of dominance, aggression, all that. Fine.

"But this doesn't mean such a pup is any more healthy than the shy pup. Nor does it mean a shy dog is undesirable as a pet. Maybe the owner wants something he can handle, something gentle. Maybe a considerate owner knows the dog will spend most of his life alone, and a pup with fire will eventually burn a hole through the furniture, or fold from boredom."

Looking for the Sick Pup

"Now, how do you tell if the pup is sick?" Doc continues. "Lots of ways. That pup has to have bright, clear eyes. A smooth, slick coat.

This cocker pup's eyes tell us, "I don't know if I trust this guy or not." But he should—it's Dr. Dick Royse.

A clean muzzle and nose. Beware of the pup who has a discharge from the nose or one who's drooling around the mouth.

"The pup should stand erect on his feet, not splayed out, not coon-footed, as we call it. He should be clean. I mean physically clean. He shouldn't have feces all over him. He shouldn't be messy. He shouldn't stink."

Doc raises the pipe stem toward the kitchen ceiling. The coffeepot quits gulping, so I know it's perked. I pour the black stuff and Doc continues, "Turn the pup over. Look at his tummy. He shouldn't have any red spots, skin eruptions, or pustules [pimples]. That tummy should be very smooth and, at weaning age, slightly pink.

"If there's a discharge from the penis of a male pup, you may or may not have to worry about it. The prepuce [foreskin] is like a dirt scoop. It's forward and it's got a slit in it, and every time that pup lays down on the ground or runs through the grass, he can pick up a little dirt or pollen in that prepuce opening. And it's just common bacteria that will develop in there. It's a local problem instead of systemic [not an infection of the system].

"The puppy should be in good flesh, like thoroughbred horses look in fancy paintings. You shouldn't see his ribs sticking out. He should be solid in your hand, the more dense the better.

"Observe the skin closely for any eruptions under the hair. Run your hand against the lay of the hair. Look for sores or scaliness. Observe if this puppy or his littermates sit around and scratch a lot, dig at their ears."

The pipe's held motionless as Doc tests the coffee cup to see if the brew is cooled. He says, "Now if this pup has a potbelly, try to see if it's in perspective. Sure, if you get to the kennel ten minutes after feeding, all the pups look bloated. But if you've got a puppy who is all tummy, yet his ribs are sticking out and his backbone shows, be suspicious. He may be heavily parasitized [got worms].

"If there's feces smeared on the underside of the tail, and below the rectum and below the haunches, that puppy has to have diarrhea. Could be parasitized. Because there's about three or four types of main parasites that cause soft stools.

"Check the color of the pup's mucous membranes. Lift up his lip and pull down his lower eyelid; that skin should be a bright, healthy pink. But on dark-skinned dogs these membranes can be pigmented toward liver, and that's all right. But if the skin's blanched-out white, either on the gums or on the conjunctiva (eyelid liner), beware of anemia.

"What I'm saying is if that pup shows a potbelly, or anemia, or diarrhea, then you're looking at three good indications he's got worms.

"Now look for an umbilical hernia. Make sure there's not a little cleft or bubble at the belly button. Now if that hernia is very large on a bitch who's going to be bred, that bubble may herniate when she's pregnant.

"Now check the bite. If the pup's parrot-mouthed so he can't scoop feed out of the pan, you've got trouble."

Doc jams a finger in the pipe to compress the black tobacco. This smoking is a Sunday pastime. He says, "It's hard to say anything about a pup's joints. They're all awkward. Obviously, a pup shouldn't limp. He should track well (back feet should follow the front). He should not be weak in his hindquarters or sway from one side to the other. But beware of extremely enlarged joints. In other words, if the puppy looks like he's knobby at his carpals or wrists or elbows or hocks, that may mean he has rickets. But we don't see much of that anymore with the new commercial puppy foods.

"However, on a big dog, ask the breeder if both sire and dam have OFA (Orthopedic Foundation for Animals) certification that attests to the absence of hip dysplasia."

ASKING QUESTIONS

"Matter of fact, there's a lot of questions you want to ask the breeder. Is he maintaining an ongoing heartworm check in his kennels? Ask if he's wormed the pups. Ask how many times. Ask what kind of shots he's given for distemper, hepatitis, leptosporosis, parvo. Now there's so much confusion about this. What is a puppy shot? It's a serum and it'll last a pup about two and a half weeks. Whereas a permanent shot is a vaccine that can give the dog lifetime immunity, though some vets like to tighten that defense up with occasional boosters."

A Clean Bill of Health

"Then, Bill, the breeder must be told you're buying this pup only on a clean bill of health from your vet. A reputable breeder will want to know the results." Doc sighs and says, "But who gets to talk to the breeder anymore? There's too many of these doggy-in-the-window impulse purchases. Heck, people pick up a pup on a whim somewhere between a shopping-center purchase and their way to the parking lot. It's the old thing of getting home with a goldfish and then finding you don't have a bowl for it.

"What everyone must realize when taking in a pup is that they're adopting a new member of the family. A mighty important member. A pet's not a whatnot for a shelf. A pet's a living, expressing, reacting being, and he requires medical care, schooling, housing, feeding, exercise, love.

"But back to picking. Look for fleas. You can see them running on the bare underbelly. Anybody can find a tick. Ear mites? Look in the ear for dirt and waxy debris. Take a sniff. Mites cause a stink.

"How about mange? If a pup sits around scratching a lot and you're thinking fleas but can't find 'em, maybe the pup's got a subtle mange. But if that pup's got sarcoptic mange and you carry him home, your other pets will get it, too.

"And distemper's something else you can take home. People look for this, but they usually don't know the symptoms. They lift a pup, and he upchucks. 'Distemper,' they say. Hardly. Pups vomit easily, what with their scavenging habits and voracious eating.

"So what do you look for? Lethargy, runny and pussy eyes, a snotty nose, quite often a dry, short, hacking cough, usually a loss of body weight, a poor appetite or no appetite at all. And how can you judge appetite with a litter running around? You can't. So head for the vet first. First and foremost.

"Otherwise, you may not be buying pleasure at all. You may be paying money for a pup's pain, your pain, and a fistful of problems. All of which could have been avoided. If you want a sick pup, that means you want to be a sick-pup nurse.

"And that's not what people want, Bill," says Doc as he steps outside and knocks out the pipe in his palm. "They want a buddy, not a bed case."

9

Getting Pup Settled In

This guy came to the farm and bought a Lab pup. He walked to his car, lifted the trunk lid, and started to stow the pup. I asked, "What are you doing?" The guy told me, "I'm taking him home . . . I don't want him to wet in the car." I walked over, handed the guy his check, took the pup, and said, "You gonna start him in a black hole? That's the way he'll live his life with you. Get the hell out of here!"

If you're going to adopt a dog then start thinking dog. Dogs don't know a Mercedes from a buckboard . . . and don't care. All a car means to them is a window to slobber on, a place to bark at the adjacent car waiting at the intersection, somewhere to go nuts when they see a horse or a dog alongside the road.

Tinkle? I've got a six-year-old Isuzu Trooper out there in the garage. It's been upchucked on, pooped on, tinkled on, and it's still mint in my eyes. How? The back platform is covered with blankets and towels. They wash easy.

The dogs are happy, the arrangement is carefree, the dogs are not put down, and we have a ball touring town.

No coupe, sedan, or sports car is fit for Pup. He must have a recreational vehicle or station wagon with a *broad platform.* For big dogs, I go to the janitorial-supply house and buy a rubber runner. Lay it the length of the platform and let some hang over. Drop that excess over the wagon door when loading and you'll avoid scratched paint.

But if the family car is all you've got, then take a cardboard box stuffed with towels to deliver Pup home.

Introducing Pup

If there are other dogs in the house, then exit the car holding Pup high. Let the family sniff him, then slowly lower him to their domain. Oftentimes the pup is intimidated. Why not? But Candy, weighing two pounds, shouldered her way through five adults, and that was the start of something grand.

Give Pup the Run of the House

Once inside, let Pup explore. Let him sniff. Even let him tinkle—I'll tell you how to clean it up. But first, pup-proof the place.

If a pup chews an electrical cord, he can electrocute himself. Place all cords atop tables—or spray with Bitter Apple bought at any pet supply store. Pups will chew whatever they find. I was talking to a lady in New Mexico last night. She told me a horror story. Her dalmatian found a child's balloon in the yard and ate it. The attached string severed his intestine, and the dog died. No matter how careful you are with Pup, calamity can even fall from the skies.

Dogs have been known to die from lapping antifreeze on a garage floor. Buddy Smith, a gun-dog trainer in Tennessee, told me three days ago two of his star prospects found antifreeze in a field where thieves had stripped a car. The dogs died. Avoid contact with anything toxic.

Even to this extent. Dee told me of a lady in one of her stores yesterday who reported that her westie walked through some antifreeze on the street and licked his paws only when he returned home. The westie died.

Keep doors shut on all cupboards that hold household cleansers. Death also awaits in the home.

Gather up and put away any doilies you have covering tables where part of the fabric hangs down. That's as tempting for a pup as a hanging awning is for a teenager. Same with throw rugs—especially those with tassels.

The best toy a pup can have is a house slipper: scent, sight, taste, gum stimulation, teething, all that good stuff. But wait! A house slipper can look just like your best pair of street shoes. Make sure your closet door is kept closed.

If you've got dining room chairs with rungs low and parallel to the floor then spray them with Bitter Apple (a store-bought repellent), for if not, I can assure you Pup is going to chew them good.

And there has never been a house with young kids where one of them didn't come running to Mother bawling about Pup stealing their favorite toy. It will just happen. Matter of fact, Pup needs tons of toys of his own. They keep him interested, preoccupied, provide gum stimulation, good teething, oral satisfaction, and make him adroit in handling objects.

THE FLYSWATTER

Occasionally you'll have a pup who eats feces. What a disgusting practice! Break it fast. Bellow with the voice and give a tap (I said tap: The purpose is symbolic, not to hurt) with a flyswatter, saying, "No, no, no, no!" and managing the most ferocious face you can make. (The flyswatter will be discussed in detail later.)

You know how animals display? Birds expand their neck ruffs to appear larger. Have you watched a turkey erect his tail? Looks formidable, right? Snakes hiss and flick their tongues. Lions lift their manes and roar. So you do the same thing. Display. Pup will get the message.

Or, in other words, train like Momma dog does. She is all mock malice, a hot breath of opprobrium, standing directly over the errant pup and breathing down hard, glaring with slit eyes, a guttural growl; it's all a show. Get to acting.

Coprophagy

Some experts say Pup eats feces out of boredom. That's not always so. In a family of, say, eight dogs, why would only one have this disgusting need? All eight dogs are bombarded with the same stimuli. The dogs are not bored.

It can be argued the feces provides some nutritional need. Bosh. Every dog is equally well fed.

So why do they do it? Once again, folks, we just don't know. And I've asked easily a thousand experts to give us this very answer.

But I'll tell you this: There's a way to break this nauseating practice—for an older dog. Let's say an eighteen-month-old pup just never has quit chewing or digging or eating stools. Then get a spray can of cayenne pepper and leave all feces in the yard for one day. (Use Bitter Apple for puppies. Pepper spray is a very severe deterrent.) Go to each deposit and spray with pepper. Pup will make his rounds, get a whiff of that, and he'll be hard-pressed to ever go back and sniff again. Unless he's very hardheaded. Like the recent overpopulation of bears entering towns and knocking over trash cans. Pepper-sprayed garbage does not deter them.

Do *not* spray Pup with the pepper: It could be absolute torture in his eyes. Yet, as you will learn when breaking up a fight between extraordinarily large and tenacious dogs, the seriousness of the fight warrants a direct-face spray. This is one case where it's best to hurt the dog, because otherwise he may be killed in the fight.

The pepper spray I use says it's 10 percent pepper by volume with an ultraviolet identifying dye. But that 10 percent is actually oleoresin capsicum derived from any of the red peppers in the nightshade family.

I've asked several vets about the benefits of putting a couple of drops of anise or monosodium glutamate (MSG), in Pup's food. I've been told these additives give stool a taste that repels dogs. But this practice is so new no one has an opinion on it.

Nor do we know much about the deficiency of a digestive enzyme called amylase. I've heard if a dog's low on that, he'll eat feces.

So the cure goes: Put a teaspoon of papain in Pup's food and he may stop considering feces.

For a young pup spray the feces, plus the pup's mouth, with Bitter Apple. It works. And it is much milder than pepper. Pepper spray would be way too harsh for a pup under eighteen months of age.

Make Sure Pup Knows

Too many dogs are corrected, but they don't know what for. Say Pup is pulling your laundry from the line and you yell, "No, Pup . . . come here!" And when Pup comes running to you, you beat the hell out of him. Now why does Pup think you hurt him? It's quite evident in his mind: Because he came to you. So he vows he'll never come to you again if you call. Now you're going to have muddy laundry in the dirt and a runaway pup. Oh, what a trainer!

The reason I emphasize this is twofold. When you see Pup doing something wrong, *that's* your best opportunity for training. Get to him fast, bellowing, "No, no, no, no!" and *point to the source of the problem* and do whatever you find best according to the situation. Now there's no doubt in Pup's mind why he's being corrected. You caught him in the act; the evidence is before him; he's caught and knows it. That's why close surveillance is necessary in starting out a pup. When he stops to tinkle, you see it, you know it, you show it, and you yell out and grab him up and go out the back door. Pup knows. Just a few times like this, and he's yours.

This is especially the fact in potty and tinkle breaking.

For it's just this simple. Pup knows that you go nuts when he dumps in the house. But outdoors you coo to him and praise him and clap your hands and smile a lot. His reaction? "Inside that house is the last place I'll ever dump." Why? Well, Pup didn't learn because of the act; he learned because of the place. Remember: Place is very important to Pup and always will be. *Always use place to train.*

ANOTHER WAIF

Once again I visited the vet to be handed a hardship pet. This time it's a Lhasa boy pup. I'll train him up to fit in a nice home—he'll leave here with his Ph.D. Oh, incidentally, remember the one-eyed rabbit I was handed in the first chapter of this book? We found a home for him with five-year-old Joshua Scharfencamp of Cottonwood, Arizona. His parents built a rabbit pen next to Joshua's bedroom and cut a hole in the wall so the rabbit could come and go.

This new Lhasa is only six weeks old, which means he left the nest at five weeks: unheard of! And he came down from the mountains,

With mud caked on his nose, Champ tells me: "This is the way you dig a hole." As deep as he succeeded in digging, I must agree with him.

whelped by a horse wrangler, to end up in a metro home with a child who just didn't know how to handle him. The pup is terrified.

So now I have this tyke who runs sideways upon hearing noise and has a temper to put Satan in his hole.

Well, that's the kind of challenge that tests us. But it all proves easy, for this Lhasa is extremely bright. In four days (using the material you have in this book), Champ (with what he's gone through, he's earned the name) knows how to use the doggy door, the command "no, no, no, no, no!" his name, the yard, the personality of each of the house dogs (who'll nip him, and who won't), where I put his food bowl down, and how to go up and down the stairs. (Possibly, folks, the greatest asset a pup can have is intelligence. It makes all training so much easier. One way to test intelligence in a whelping kennel is to see which pup can follow you out a gate. Most pups will get hung up on the gate panel and never see the opening to the outside. The one who walks through the opening is the one you should take home.)

He also knows when I put him in his dog crate, high up on the chair beside my bed, he is to be quiet and go to sleep.

And later he'll learn to use the ramp to get on the bed: We bought this ramp for Muffy because, with her bad back, she couldn't jump.

Dee's on the road so this pup is left for me to make a good house guest—though Dee could do it so much better. Women are excellent with pups.

Know this: Just when you think your pup is the brightest guy (or gal) who ever lived, there'll come a day, even a week, when he'll seem to have suffered a lobotomy. He won't remember a thing. Endure. And start all over.

WHAT PUP LOVES MOST

There are things about the house that every pup loves. Take dirty clothes. No other bed means so much: Let them have the pile. (Remember scent?) There's never been a table leg that didn't finally get Pup's attention—and too often, his teeth marks. Produce the fly-swatter, get your mean face on, and your threatening voice, then after the correction is past, spray the table leg with Bitter Apple. Or, in tough cases, with older dogs, spray pepper.

You can go one better with Bitter Apple than just spraying the furniture. If Pup flat won't quit, then spray his mouth. He'll absolutely hate this. Fine. That's what we want: to deter him. Take him to the chewed leg, spray the leg—all the time saying "no, no, no!" then turn right around and spray Pup's opened mouth (not his eyes, for God's sake). Now Pup *knows* that table leg is more trouble than it's worth. He's standing there looking at it . . . and tasting the horrible consequences.

Sure, all of this is a lot of bother, but no one said raising a pup was carefree. You get a lot back from this little guy in the house; expect to pay your dues.

Pups love to roll and scootch in grass, so have some small patches of it in your backyard. Sure, they eat some. Everybody's got a theory why they do it, but no one really knows why. What's important to realize is this: I've never known a dog to die from grass ingestion. You should know this, however. It is argued rather logically that Pup eats the grass because the rough edges scratch some irritant in his throat. Others note that wild dogs do not go only for meat when they make a kill. They also go for a salad—their prey usually grazes on greens—in the stomach. This grass eating, then, may be an atavistic impulse for Pup.

THAT SPECIAL PLACE

Every dog has a favorite place in a home. Pup will eventually find where he wants to spend his spare time. Usually it's under something. Dogs fear anything above them. That's why you'll see the house dog sleeping under the coffee table, farm dogs under porches.

Also, dogs are very sensitive to temperature. Lhasas came from high Tibet (they didn't enter America until 1933) and they hate hot weather. So they spread flat-bellied on house tile, linoleum, wood, concrete. Anyplace that is cool. Then there's the opposite need in winter: Pups will sleep in front of the fireplace, on the carpeting, and especially close to their human partner in bed. Don't think they can't find out who's got the electric blanket turned on.

BEDDY-BYE TIME

That first night you bring Pup home can be a pain. There's nothing more irritating than a yelping pup, so why have one? Get a kennel crate up on a chair, or a baby pen—something Pup can see out of, *and see you,* and put it immediately next to your bed. That's it. Pup will see you and sleep the night. To help him settle in, you can dress him in a sweater, or a covered hot-water bottle, if it's winter (he just came from Mom, who kept him warm); give him an alarm clock that ticks so he'll associate that sound with his mother's heartbeat; provide a medium-sized stuffed toy for Pup to cuddle up against; and expect the possibility of wet towels in the morning so put baby pads on the crate floor.

But isolate Pup in the utility room, and you'll have pandemonium all night long.

KEEPING A CLEAN CRATE

Pups don't want to foul their nest. Oops! That used to be the case before shopping-mall pets. Those pups are born, transported, and raised in crates. That's where they eat, sleep, tinkle, and dump. Put something soft (like a towel or a quilt) in the crate. Just this change of flooring will often start Pup off dry and keep him that way—along with your close monitoring.

But non-shopping-mall pups generally won't tinkle in the enclosed crate if they can help it—regardless of the flooring. Consequently, come dawn, get up and out fast. Get Pup to the yard and praise him for tinkling. Really lay it on thick.

Now it's really tough to house-train a pup in a two-story house. You've got a long way to descend. So, in the beginning, when Pup's in his infancy, carry him all the way outside and put him down in the same spot each time.

But later put Pup down so he can descend the stairs on his own and know this: *He's going to stoop to wet when he hits the first-floor carpet.* But you're ready. If you are nimble, stay in front of him and cheer him along. If stoved up, then touch his bottom with your toe and, saying "no," keep him moving. You'll make it to the yard, and there won't be a mistake.

Also, when you must leave the house for a short time, put Pup in his crate. He'll try not to tinkle while you're gone.

Sooner than you think, Pup will housebreak himself. He'll know he tinkles or dumps only when in the yard, and you can put the crate away.

THE MELLOW PRO

But I must tell you about a professional gun-dog trainer named Gary Ruppel of Parker, Colorado. Gary takes pups to bed with him in their infancy. He says he's a light sleeper and when the pup stirs, Gary gets him out of the house. He says pups are inclined to whimper in the crate, but a pup in bed just goes to sleep with never a murmur.

FEEDING

Pup must have his own place to eat with no intruders. Of course the other dogs are going to be curious and will probably bother him. Just stand by and monitor all the goin's-on—we don't want Pup frightened. The best way to handle this feeding is to isolate Pup. Buy an expandable, portable gate, and put him in a room by himself. It works wonders, and the gate can go anywhere with you.

If you've whelped a litter and the pups are five weeks old or so, you can supplement Mother's milk by using powdered milk. Why?

Muffy checks the plans for our new house. She's told me that her eating area must be larger so no one bothers her.

Because you can determine the consistency by how much water you add. Place some kibbles made specifically for infant pups in the bowl. Also, chop up some meat from a canned dog food (one of the starter kind) at least three times a day. Mix it all together and make a gruel.

Now let me say this fast. There are many vets who will challenge all I've said. Their point is: The manufacturers are now putting out so many quality formulas for every-aged dog that all my mixin' and goin' on is unnecessary. Their point is well taken: You must avoid supplements and treats. Well, I'll answer that. There were many of us mixin' infant food long before the dog-food manufacturers saw the possibility of making millions by preparing specific formulas.

Whatever you feed, always provide ample water (good health for dogs requires three times as much water as food). Too many dogs die of kidney failure, so keep Pup flushed out. Kidney failure is the second cause of canine death, preceded only by cancer, and followed by heart disease.

And let there be a rawhide strip (a caution follows later) for Pup to chew on to strengthen his teeth and massage his gums, and to satisfy his chewing craving (better that than a chair leg). Try not to give a factory-processed, cereal-based food treat (much more about this, too). I know it's tempting to offer some specially processed food tidbit you found at the pet store. Just don't do it for the time being. I'll tell you why later.

TOILET TRAINING

There's nothing to housebreaking a pup. First off, you should install a doggy door. That way Pup can come and go on his own terms; he doesn't have to wait for you. Which further means Pup enters the outdoor world through that door, so he must have a fenced-in backyard.

But here's what usually happens. You're watching TV and you notice Pup suddenly start to run, then spin. Bolt up, grab Pup, and head out. Pup's telling you it's coming. Make for the backyard.

Now, once there, take Pup to the same spot every time and tell him to tinkle or potty—or whatever words you prefer. This is important. For yes, telling Pup what to do will eventually trigger him to dump on command. And about that spot? Eventually Pup will find his own spot . . . then that's where you put him down.

Never be rough with Pup on housebreaking. Always be gentle, relaxed, joyful. Make it a good game. When Pup does his business, praise him, stoop over and point to what he did and tell him what a good boy he is. Yes, Pup will grow to understand. He will sense your feeling more than acknowledge your words. Always remember: FIDO.

But there are times you are going to have trouble. Many pups don't want to go out in the rain or snow or wind. That's why we started the vocal commands. Pup's out there shivering and wanting to go back in. But what about you? You're wet, it's cold, and Pup's doin' nothing. Well, encourage him, talk to him, tell him exactly what you want him to do. Walk him to another spot to trigger him.

Should you have other dogs, take Pup to where one just tinkled; that should stimulate him. This rain and snow is one reason you'll want a patio roof outside your back door that extends over a patch of gravel. With such protection, Pup will not get wet nor have to climb over a snow mound. And the gravel will trigger him to dump.

If you're around home all day, then take Pup out every two hours. Think for him. But alas, what of the working guy or gal in an apartment? You don't want the carpet soaked? Okay, put Pup in the bathroom or utility room and close him off with an expandable gate—any type of gate Pup can see through. He'll not feel isolated. Put down towels and do the laundry each night.

MAKING A HOUSE FIT FOR A DOG

And finally, put down the right flooring and you won't even know Pup lives there. I'm talking, for example, about Mexican Saltillo tile. Drip urine on it, or have a dog's water bowl splash out, and the adobe absorbs it. A bachelor could go for years without ever mopping up. Stains just don't show.

And then there's Berber carpeting. Get it in a speckled tan or brown with a prominent ridge pattern. It'll be hard to find the place Pup tinkled even when you watched him do it.

A PLACE TO SLEEP

Now, once Pup is trained in all these things, where is he to sleep? This is after he's graduated from the elevated crate by your bed. Well, let him pick the place; then you fix it up for him.

If it's your own bed, that's fine with me, but you've got to make up your own mind. Wherever you put him, let him have access to you. Too many dogs are frightened of thunder—don't lock him up and make him quake all night isolated from you.

If bonded, you and Pup will have the same mind and heart. How's that to happen when he's kept far away?

CLEANING UP WHAT PUP PUTS DOWN

If Pup stools on your carpet or wets on your sofa, it's not the end of the world. There are ways to take care of this that are both carefree and effective.

Let's take upchuck. That's got grease in it. So we want a grease cutter. Use a paper towel to pick up the residue. Scrub with a wet bath towel or clean rag. Drop two Alka-Seltzer tablets in a glass of warm water and pour the drink on the spot. Blot up. Now, should there still be a spot, then use any of the following solutions—they all work: Resolve, diluted vinegar, PDQ, Simple Solution, and Clear Choice.

Now, there may be one thing wrong with every one of these products, except the vinegar. Being cleansing solutions they may, of themselves, leave a residue. And some residues will collect dust and discolor. So what to do? Just get a pan of water, saturate the spot you just treated, and scrub with a large towel. Remove any suds left by the commercial cleaners. You'll finally have a clean carpet again.

When traveling with a vomiting pup in a car, buy a plastic dropcloth. Costs a buck. Load your wagon platform then cover with the plastic cloth and cover again with a blanket.

Now should Pup upchuck, his vomitus won't penetrate the plastic cloth and get on what you're transporting as well as the car's interior.

Should this happen, though, there are two things you can do. One: Flush and work out with a cleanser. Or two: Let dry and whisk away with a hard-bristled scrub brush.

As for tinkle, everything above applies. However, first off, take a wad of paper towels and press them into the wet spot with your shoe sole or butt of your hand. Do it over and over until you get no imprint. Now go to your Resolve, et cetera. Then, later, flush with lots of water. And soak up with a large bath towel. If one treatment doesn't do the job, then repeat.

When you have feces on the carpet pick it up with tissue and flush it down the toilet. Treat as above.

With diarrhea, take a knife and scrape the residue onto a piece of cardboard and throw it in the trash. Or just leave it, let it dry, then scrape it up. You can help it dry by smothering it with salt. Salt is a desiccating agent. The diarrhea will dry, and you can clean.

But what are you going to do with feces left in the yard? Buy yourself a pair of scoop tools. One serving as a repository, the other as a rake. For grass, gravel, or concrete, make sure the rake has teeth. Now go around each morning and scoop up. If you live in a moderately dry climate, you can leave a cardboard box in the backyard with a black garbage bag in it. Gather the bag up once each week and send it away with the trash pickup. If your climate is wet, then use a galvanized pail with a lid for a container, and once again put a garbage-can liner inside.

I've tried every disposal system known to man one time or another. You'll read about a tank you put in a pit where you deposit the feces and treat with lime. Forget it. I never saw such a mess.

The best system I ever had was on the farm, where I'd use an auger on the power takeoff to drill holes in the fields. That was great.

THE COLOR YELLOW

There are two spots that can defeat you. To remove them, you must catch them fast. That's a yellow-bile upchuck or a loose yellow stool. The color yellow is your enemy. Get busy fast and use everything in your cleansing arsenal. But if Pup upchucks at midnight and you don't catch it until morning—you're in for trouble.

Same with bright yellow urine. Got a dog who won't drink sufficient water? You'll get a yellow spot. Work hard and fast.

Each time a new pup eats, awakens, or drinks, he should be taken outdoors. Remember this: It's your responsibility.

But there is one salvation to the color yellow: Rent and use a carpet cleaner, follow instructions, and often—even weeks later—the yellow will disappear. I find it amazing.

Caught in the Act

So what if Pup doesn't make it outside and you just step into a puddle? Well, you didn't see him do it, so all you can do is call him to you, point to the spot, and tell him "no." Then start cleaning. Oftentimes Pup will watch you. Fine, as you're working keep telling him in a soft but disappointed voice, "no, no, no."

But what's this? You come around the corner, and there Pup is tinkling. Now you can let out a scream. You caught him in the act.

Pup'll be startled, stop, and maybe start to run. Scoop him up, telling him "no, no, no!" and carry him out to his favorite spot. Let him see the disappointment in your face, hear it in your voice, smell it in your breath. Let him smell the chemistry of anger released by your body. Let him sense the hot aura of you.

Just when you think he'll never catch on, Pup'll be trained. And it won't take long.

Never Get Mad

But don't ever get mad. *If a dog makes you mad, he's defeated you.* Remember this—because one maniacal act can destroy Pup forever. Besides, you can take the spirit out of a pup, but you can't put it back in. So avoid all this through self-discipline. We judge dogs, you know. They pass or fail the test. But I've often said it's a shame there's not a panel of dogs serving as judges to judge the trainers. Trainers fail to pass the test, too. Put a score on yourself from Pup's point of view.

In this regard, I like to recall the greatest dog handler of all time. He was Clyde Morton of Sedgefields Plantation near Alberta, Alabama. Clyde is the only man to win the National Bird Dog Championship eleven times. And I just left talking to his sister, Mrs. Eloise Meagher, and her daughter, Mrs. Paula Sensing, both of Memphis, Tennessee.

Well, one day, they tell me, Clyde was working a dog in the presence of his niece when the man was made instantly furious. But what did Clyde do?

He slid from his horse, abandoned it, walked slowly to a shade tree, put his back to it, and slid down. There he sat a long time looking off to the far distance and trying to gain an equal and shallow breath.

His niece asked him, "What happened, Uncle Clyde?"

And Uncle Clyde replied—and get this, you must get this—"If I had touched that dog, I would have ruined him. *It was more important I get control of myself than control of that dog.*"

HEALTH, HEALTH, HEALTH

Finally, keep Pup on schedule at the vet. Make sure the clinic makes up a shot card for you to keep. And, hopefully, you've chosen an outfit that'll send you postcard reminders telling when what dog is due for what booster. We're going to talk a lot about the client-dog-vet relationship in this book—so we'll leave the rest of our vet concerns for later.

10

Living with Our Dogs

While backpacking in the mountains, I met a shepherd working sheep. Now, folks, I've been invited as a guest to the International Sheep Dog Championships in Great Britain, worked sheep on the Scottish Highlands, and driven rank cattle off the greasewood flats of Texas with border collies. But I never saw a performance like this guy with his one-year-old pup in my life. So I asked him, "How did you train this dog?" And the man laughed when he said, "Train him? I'm not a trainer . . . he just follows me wherever I go."

Dog training?

You don't need it.

There are only three basic commands to get your dog through life and to have you stay content. They are his name, "no," and "come here." You don't need any more.

And why is this? Well, if a dog will come when you call him and stop what he's doing when you say "no," then that's a perfectly trained dog. One who can participate with you in anything you ever want to do in life.

So let's examine these three commands.

Name your dogs something with a consonant that can be

slammed against the teeth. Tug, the name of the male westie, was excellent. For you're going to yell this name to keep Pup from bounding into the street, running off with the steak that fell from the barbecue, or frightening some meter reader.

I've noticed for the past thirty-five years that the name of the dog has essentially become my only command. Dogs soon learn what every predicament requires, what behavior is off-limits, what you want them to be doing. Just say their name, and they'll comply (and the rest of the house pack will ignore you). Seldom is this name used for the expression of love: You'll find yourself coming up with an intimacy. Sugar becomes Sugie when I'm telling her how beautiful she is. Somehow Muffy became known as Momma to Dee, then Moomoo, and finally MoMo. Muff answers to all of them. Dee and her words.

God, I was proud of Muffy this morning. She's had so much medical treatment and I pulled up to the vet—she has to hate the place—and she asked to be let out, then led me to the door without a leash, and entered. I've never seen a more valiant gal. Her sense of duty is overwhelming, and this is another dog who was never trained. Dee and I just talked to her, and kept her with us every minute of the day, and loved her.

Well, anyway, if your dog will come when you call him then all your problems are solved. Take Tiffany. She wants to bark (which is the worst part of a Lhasa). And she turns me off when I tell her not to. So what do I do? I ask her to come here. She leaves off with the barking to come get her ears scratched. Then I tell her in a soft voice, "No, that's not what we do." She looks at me. It's hard for her to grasp things readily. Then she wanders off, there's no more barking, and I didn't end up yelling at a dog.

There'll be a day Tiff won't bark when I tell her, "Knock off that noise."

And another thing I noticed this morning. Instead of telling Sugar (who was under the breakfast table) to knock it off because she wanted to growl at the two wrestling twins, I merely brushed the hair on her back toward her neck with my bare foot. Now, no way did I ever use this technique to train Sugar to do anything. But she stopped growling. Dogs just know. *Sugar sensed what I wanted her to do: FIDO.*

After you've lived with your dog(s) several years, no words, gestures—nothing—are needed anymore to communicate one to the other.

You learn to feel what the other wants.

And remember this: In the old way of training, the dog obeyed out of fear.

Our method gets compliance from the bonded dog because he doesn't want to disappoint us.

The first is negative, the second positive. The first requires force on your part, the latter love. In the first instance, you train with intimidation. In the latter method you train with intimacy.

Do you mind reading the above three paragraphs again? They're the most important words in this book.

So How Do You Get a Pup to Come?

Start young. Start everything young. Dr. J. Paul Scott, senior scientist and director of the Animal Behavior Research Program at Hamilton Station near Bar Harbor, Maine, discovered the concept of "critical periods" in the life of a puppy. Dr. Scott studied such things as when a puppy can start to learn, how long he requires his mother's care, when his brain reaches adult maturity so he can start learning adult requirements, and when his behavior pattern crystalizes, characterizing the dog's personality and actions for the rest of his life.

Dr. Scott learned that every puppy's life is divided into definite periods, and some of these periods are more important than others. Especially significant is three weeks of age, when a puppy suddenly begins to learn as quickly and efficiently as an adult. In addition, now he begins socializing, which determines his subsequent relations with human partners and dogs for the rest of his life.

From two to three weeks, the puppy cuts his first tooth, begins to walk, wags his tail, and has increased electrical activity within his brain. Within this seven-day period, the infant is transformed into a puppy.

Dr. Scott learned that the puppy may leave the care of his mother at seven weeks of age and have the ability to learn whatever can be taught in short lessons. If a pup is neglected from three weeks to sixteen weeks of age, he will be so impaired that he will never recover; he will never make a traditional pet.

Within a short time, Dr. Scott was joined by Clarence Pfaffenberger, a counsel to the American Kennel Club who was sought out by the Guide Dog–founding ladies in California to help with dog selection and preparation.

Extending Dr. Scott's research, Pfaffenberger learned that if a pup would not fetch a ball after five weeks of training, he would never make a guide dog because he had little innate desire to please people.

Pfaffenberger also learned that if a break in training occurred for a puppy, but if he was placed in a good home within one week, this pup had a 90 percent chance of succeeding as a guide dog. But if that interim period was three weeks, the puppy had only a 30 percent chance of success. This indicates the absolute need of pups for continual human contact, stimulation, and love.

Additional breakthroughs by these two researchers were equally startling and beneficial.

Dogs are not trained with a clock. Admittedly, working dogs are trained in a structured program where each day sees some new link added to their chain of knowledge and performance.

But that's not the way with house dogs. They proceed at their own pace. And never is there a structured training session. Oh, yes, if you want to get a collar and rope and go out back for heel, sit, stay, I'll go with you; but honest, folks, it ain't needed.

For example, the working-dog trainer will collar the dog and snap on a leash or check cord. Then he'll stand distant, call the dog's name to get his attention, say, "Come here," and give the cord a jerk. The dog will rise and come forward, or the trainer will milk him in, hand over hand, on the check cord.

Or the dog will object and sullen up, and the trainer will have to drag him across the lawn. Or the dog will go nuts and leap and tug and carry on like a marlin on a fishing line. And you'll recall, folks: This dog just experienced something bad he can associate directly with a human being. Which can never, never happen. Remember?

We don't want any of this.

COME HERE

So this is the way we start teaching "come here." You're sitting in the living room, or at the kitchen table, and you see Pup appear—he's walking toward you. Fine. Tell him, "Come here." You're giving Pup a command for what he's already doing. Keep it up, day after day. Oh, yes, don't forget to whistle.

Then lie on the floor and say, "Come here." Pup will come leaping, for dogs love to have humans on the floor available for their tongue, nose, and paws.

Then throw a ball. Pup will chase it, and you're still on the floor, telling him, "Come here." When he returns, praise him. Make it a joyous game.

But know this. If Pup brings the ball back, never, never grab it and pull it from his clenched jaws. That makes a hardmouthed dog. A dog who may one day have your newspaper and shred it as you try to take it away.

So you never pull a ball, you push a ball. That's right. Grab the ball, shove it into the wedge of Pup's jaw (which makes him gag), and twist (which breaks Pup's tooth-hold on the ball). Or, get down and blow an abrupt blast of air into Pup's nose. Or, standing over him, take the ball in one hand as you reach over and place your pointing finger under the flap of skin leading from Pup's hind leg toward his stomach. Now pull. The discomfort will prompt Pup to open his mouth and drop the ball.

But never, never pull anything from a young pup's mouth, be it a towel, toy, bone, ball, shoe, or anything whatsoever. And only when he's older can you use the techniques mentioned above.

Commanding Pup to Do What He's Doing

So whatever Pup is doing, give that command. Pup starts to sit. Tell him to do just that: "Sit." He starts to run away, tell him, "Hie on," which is the command to go away. He starts to enter his crate which is on the floor, tell him, "Kennel."

Now go out back. When Pup's distant, tell him, "Come here." If he ignores you, throw a ball. When he fetches it up, say, "Come here." He may bring it to you, and he may not.

If Pup ignores you and he's holding the ball in his mouth, turn your back to him. Pups can't stand this. They won't accept rejection. Besides, they want to be the star; they want all your attention. Seeing your back, Pup will come running. When he passes by, congratulate him and get down on one knee so he'll make a circle and come back to you.

Or if Pup still doesn't come with your back turned, start running in place. Don't go anywhere, just stand there running in place. Pup will come running, for he'll think you're leaving him. Catch him as he goes by and take the ball, or leave it, as you tell him what a grand guy he is.

Or remember this. Most circus dogs are trained with food. The trainer has bits of dried liver in his pocket. Dogs love to eat. When you prepare Pup's meal, and he's distant, yell, "Hey Pup, come here." If he ignores you, tell him, "Hey Pup, it's time for nummy-nummy." Or go close to Pup's position and show him the plate of food. He'll come running as you say, "Come here."

So you see what we're doing. We're talking to Pup all the time. Sure, he doesn't know the words, but he senses the feeling we have when we speak them. And he sees all those symbols associated with what you're doing. Like the can of food, hearing the clatter of plates, your getting down to look in the cupboard for kibbles to sprinkle on the canned meat. Gradually this monitoring of symbols and sensing (FIDO) will convert to capability with language. Empathy will coexist with knowledge.

And don't think it's a long-drawn-out process. It's not—especially with a young pup. Maybe house pups learn half of all they'll ever know by the time they're a month old. I wonder. It seems that way. And by the time Pup's one year old, he'll know it all. He won't mature until he's three, and he'll know more than when he's one. But a one-year-old dog can know much: Remember the mountain shepherd and the dog who went everywhere with him?

Just now Dee left for work. She turned to Muffy and said, "Daddy will take you bye-bye." On the word "Daddy," Muffy's head jerked toward me. When Muffy heard "bye-bye," she tried to stand and start to the door. Muffy has never been in a formal training session in her life. She understands everything we say to her. I tell Muffy, "We can't go now," which prompts her to pout, but she sits down.

Now, if each of these statements were a command, how in the hell would you teach them in a structured program? You wouldn't. You teach house dogs only through intimacy, constant contact, talking, transmitting a feeling of love, and forever being patient and considerate.

STOP BARKING

I'll tell you up front Bob Wehle is the world's top dog breeder of all time. Bob's specialty is English pointers. You visit Bob's holdings in Alabama and walk down that long row of kennels where sixty dogs are housed—*and you won't hear a sound.*

I asked Bob how he did it, how he got that many dogs—dogs who are rambunctious, high-flying athletes—to not say a word. Bob stopped, smiled, and told me in soft voice, "My dogs don't bark because they don't want to disappoint me." Once again, FIDO. Dogs train themselves through feelings. Bob trains with love. He bonds

The world's top dog breeder Bob Wehle of Midway, Alabama, has redefined the English pointer.

with each of those sixty dogs so tight, they know his mind. Plus, they love Bob so much they do not want to do anything that displeases him.

Bob sells his pups all over the world. The other day a letter came in from a satisfied customer who said, "I don't understand. I got this pup and he's already trained. But I didn't do anything with him. This means he had to be genetically trained."

Bob's been raising dogs for sixty years. There's a part of the man in every litter, every prospect, every bird-dog champion. He has never swung a whip, never lifted a boot toe, never hurt a dog in any way. Bob does it all with love and kindness—does it with a breed that heretofore was known for carnal instincts, that could bolt to the next county and wipe out a coop of chickens. Bob's dogs come from the womb seemingly knowing what you're talking about, knowing what you want.

THE LOVE-TRAINED DOG

Force is the last thing that can ever be practiced in training a dog. Too many people feel the dog is insensitive and to get through they have to really whack him. But you and I know. All these dogs may be more sensitive than we humans are. Rubbing an ear accomplishes more than all the clubbing in history.

Thus the new age of dog training. We do it with a smile, a stroke, a cheery voice, a feeling (that's transmitted) of love, and a knowledge that the dog is receiving thousands of messages we don't even know we're sending: FIDO.

A dog raised this way will bond forever, will soon understand everything you say, and will seldom have to hear the deterrent "no!"

Candy is a compulsive ball player. I started throwing a tennis ball in the backyard and she began fetching it. She even became so adept that she could catch it on a hop—even with her small mouth.

Now the ball is used to communicate all sorts of things to me. Muffy and I are headed for the vet, remember? Mom told her we'd go bye-bye. Well, I've just put on my shoes and Candy appears, spitting that tennis ball at me so it bounds off my shin. Yes, she can spit that ball with uncanny accuracy. I ignore her. She wants me to pick up the ball and throw it. What she really wants is for me to acknowledge that she is there and to tell her she can go bye-bye. So here she comes back to spit the ball again. Now I tell her she can go, and the ball is dropped like a hot horseshoe.

If Candy knew how to bat, I could get $6 million a year for her from the Yankees.

You can see from all this that if dogs are given the right environment and the right attitude by their human partner, they self-train. What they come up with you'll never know.

Pooder, that long-ago mongrel terrier, began sitting on my bed each morning so she'd know when I awakened. Then she would bark me down the hall, like I was a matador being led into the ring. Dee would know we were coming and she would congratulate Pooder for getting me up and out to work. Pooder developed all this on her own. Like I say, how in the hell would you teach that?

Force: The Destroyer of Dogs

Some working-dog trainers use force methods to get results. There are many reasons. Take the gun-dog trainer: He has only so many days to produce a finished dog; the client will pay for no more. Therefore, the trainer hardly has time to bond and wait for FIDO to take hold. Therefore, all forced training is negative. Whereas all humane training is positive.

Forced training is also destructive. The dog must hand over his self-will and become a mechanical dog. And the umbrella effect of it all is intimidation, fright, stress, grudge, and loss of dignity, ingenuity, and spirit.

Many gun-dog trainers now drive their dogs by shocking them in the neck with a remote-controlled zapper. These dogs perform, no doubt about it—with their tails between their legs. Go into competition against a love-trained dog, however, and the electrically driven dog folds. I'll give you an example. A shock-trained dog, once out of sight of the handler, goes berserk. He's never been given any latitude of independence, so in an independent situation he panics. Now take the love-trained dog. His handler has already showed him that his "dog" judgment has value. So this dog has confidence. Therefore, when out of sight, he just switches into the next gear, turns on his own druthers, and gets the job done. Which dog would you want?

DOGS TRAINING DOGS

You can chisel this in marble, and it will be as true one thousand years from now as it is today: Nothing bad that happens to a pup can ever be associated with a human being. Consequently, let other dogs train pups, so that all their grudge is vented on each other.

The most classic and effective example of dogs training dogs is the litter-box check cord. I'll show you how it works.

Only the breeder can offer this service. As only the breeder can snip off the pup's dewclaws at three days of age. Now you got a slick leg that won't get hung up on something and fester.

But back to the check cord. When the litter of pups has opened their eyes, cut a bunch of 3/8-inch by 2-foot-long nylon check cords.

Tie an overhand knot in one end, wrap that end about Pup's neck, and poke it through a clinching honda in the check cord—sized to each pup's neck (see photos). This knot will not move, so there's no chance of choking Pup. The trailing cord becomes pup's leash now, and your power steering later.

Watch what happens. A pup eases about the litter box, dragging his check cord. Another pup sees the cord pass by and reaches out to slap it down with a paw, or bites it with his toothless mouth. The walking dog is suddenly stopped. "Oh Momma, Momma," he screams, "the world has come to an end . . . I can't move."

Then finally the detained pup breaks loose, and another pup comes stumbling by. This new pup is also stopped in his tracks.

My buddy Bill Berlat shows how to tie a litter box check cord. First off, tie a knot in the end. Then make a big old granny.

Now put the knotted end through the granny.

Then cinch it tight. The noose will never draw up on a pup's neck.

So what's happening? These pups are teaching each other to give to the lead. And there's no man involved. If the pup is distressed he can only look to another pup as his tormentor. Never a human being.

As the pups grow, the breeder will have to keep making a larger collar with a new check cord. Then eventually the pups will have teeth and gnaw off each other's leashes.

But the training's already been done. You walk in now, pick up a leash, and heel the pup away. Here he comes, complying, no grudge, no anger. He no longer even acknowledges the cord about his neck. This is magnificent dog training. And another dog did it.

When you train one, you train 'em all. That's what's going on with this litter of Lab pups.

THE DOG DOOR

When you install a dog door, you have to get Pup outside while you stay inside, and you get down on your knees, raise the flap, and cheer Pup to enter. And you try other techniques. But what happens if you've got a houseful of dogs who rocket through that dog door like jets? Pup follows them, and he is doorwise in five minutes.

A BAD PLACE

Now here's another law that's immutable. Dogs never forget a place where they've been hurt. Dogs associate pain with place.

Example: Happy was a young Lab I got from Queen Elizabeth. He leaped into a pond only to stroke back and drive a trot hook through his ankle. A trot hook is a big fishhook, maybe two inches long, and it hangs baited all night from a stringer in hopes of catching a catfish.

Chance Tofoya of Magdalena, New Mexico, prefers the dog door. His progress is checked by his buddy, an Australian heeler.

Well, Happy panicked. I dove in. Thrashing about, I finally cut the fishing line and got Happy to a picnic bench where I cut off the barb and slid out the hook.

So days go by. I happen to have some training dummies and Happy and I are walking along (what I call Happy Timing) and I throw the dummy into the pond where Happy got hooked. No way. Happy ain't about to enter that water. I then discover he'll lunge and cascade water on entry into any other part of the pond, but never there. That particular water is now tainted.

The obverse of this principle is also a law. Dogs associate pleasure with place. The family of Lhasas shiver when I take them to the vet, but the groomer is novel: She lets all the dogs run loose in a great room. It's like going to preschool. The dogs can't wait to get through the groomer's door.

BUT WHAT IF PUP SAYS NO?

You've met Puddin and Tiffany. With the same parents, the same genes, the same environment, Puddin and Tiff are opposites. Puddin is sweet, loving, yielding. Tiffany is pugnacious, cunning, defiant.

So we've lived together a year and both pups have come along, but they've traveled different routes. All I ever had to do was speak to Puddin to get absolute compliance.

But Tiff. No. "Voice, hell," she's saying, "it's going to take more than that to lasso me."

Well, for years I've had that little bit more. Remember? It's a flyswatter. A *white* flyswatter, so Pup can see it at a glance. You've told Pup what to do and he's turned you off. You tell him again, same result. Now you go to him (or her) and say, "You're treading on shaky ground, pardner . . . I'm going to tell you one more time, and if you don't do what I say I'm going to pop you with this flyswatter." Talk about wordy?

So, did Tiff repeatedly defy me and get hit repeatedly?

No. Just tap (and I mean tap) a pup one time with a flyswatter that you've amply displayed and forevermore, when you go get that swatter and come forward bearing it high, you've got a dog who asks where he can sign his good-citizenship papers.

One time. One tap does it, be the pup a four-pound Lhasa or a one-hundred-pound Chesapeake Bay retriever. The flyswatter becomes a symbol of your disappointment. Pup, who must have your goodwill for a good life, has lost you, has turned you against him, and the display of this swatter confirms that. Pup can't live this way. He must have your approval and your love.

For remember FIDO: exchanging messages to alter the other guy's (or dog's) behavior. Then sensing feedback to see how your message was accepted. Noting if there was compliance. But now the dog is transmitting to you with his eyes and his posture.

And what is he reading about you? More than you know you're sending. He's decoding your scent, your stance, your expression, your voice, your words, your movement. We know dogs decode us;

we just have no name for how they do it. So we have to "read" them. As novices, we go on a hunch. Only after training many dogs do we become experienced and know any facts for certain.

At any rate, there's a lot going on between man and dog at all times, and when the dog is being corrected, the message, the channels, and the feedback become extremely varied.

Jim Charlton, the golden retriever specialist from Portland, Oregon, was talking to me over the phone this afternoon and mentioned how eye contact was a major component of training. He said, "A dog will be coming back to me with a training dummy in his mouth and if I don't keep constant eye contact with him—if I divert my gaze one second, like talk to the client who owns him, and that dog has any thought of self-will—he'll quit you. He'll step over to a bush and lift a leg, he'll drop the dummy, he'll take off after a rabbit, what-have-you. But keep that eye contact intense and steady and the dog will come straight in. In effect, you bring that dog in with the power of your eyes."

To say nothing of your stance, your facial expression, your body language, your scent, your voice, and whatever tactile information you transmit.

And the display of this flyswatter is as harsh as we get in training, folks. No boot toe, no picking up the dog and slamming him, no electrical shock, no BB-loaded leather whip, no cigarette burn (yeah, it's been done), no shooting with a shotgun, slingshot, or BB gun.

Yes, many performance dogs are trained in a chamber of horrors because their trainers are totally inadequate and know nothing about dogs. As my friend Delmar Smith says, "That kind of dog trainer ain't got no fertilizer in his plot." Which means, they've got pretty sterile brains.

When You Train One You Train Them All

When I go for the flyswatter because one dog won't mind—say, Tiffany won't stop barking—the whole dog family takes off. Nine-year-old Chili tries to exit the property. Failing in that, she flees to the most distant room in the house. Chili has never been tapped by that swatter in all her life. Interesting, isn't it?

What's the Justification for the Flyswatter?

I told you Puddin was mellow, yielding, sweet. Tiffany is detached, obstinate, self-centered. Now, let's say two different households adopt each of these twins. Let's further say that the women of these homes meet at the grocery now and then and discuss their two dogs—identical dogs, twins, same blood, everything.

Puddin's owner reports, "Oh, she is the dearest thing . . . she self-trains, really. I never have to raise my voice."

The other woman is wondering what she's doing wrong, for she must report, "Tiffany won't listen to a thing I say . . . she is unruly, spiteful . . . she couldn't care less whether I like her or not."

Well, I want both women to have the best of all pets. Tiffany will yield to the flyswatter. There is some Puddin in her somewhere that will eventually take over. Now this does not, I repeat, does not, mean you beat Tiffany with the swatter. Never. And you don't have to. Just one tap accompanied with the command "no," and Tiffany is going to start reexamining her ways. Earlier this very morning, Tiffy started barking. I told her, "no." She told me to go to hell. So I grabbed the swatter and started after her. She dove under a bed. Tiffany has not barked the rest of this morning—and she wasn't touched by that flyswatter.

Without the flyswatter, what would Tiffany's human partner do? What would you do? That's the question. And that's the swatter solution.

Oh, incidentally, there is a Barker Breaker (that's the trade name) that works. When a dog barks, the breaker issues a shrill sound. Dogs hate it. And they stop barking. But what have we here? Sugar can't stand the thing. I go to turn it on prior to my leaving the house, and Sugar sees me—so off she goes under the bed. And when I come back, Sugar has tinkled in the bedroom because she will not come out so long as that breaker is activated. So sometimes you think you got a solution—you ain't got no solution at all.

But there is an old truth in dog training: You can't cure one problem without creating another. The answer, then: Don't ever create a problem in the first place.

Symbols

Dogs cue immediately to symbols, and they cue deeply. Get the leashes out, and you have a family of jumping jacks. Produce the feed bowls, and everyone crowds your legs. Bring home a new toy, and they all assemble, shoulder to shoulder, to sniff the thing. Buy a dog-training whistle and go get it—you're going to blow it to stop the barking—and if they later see that whistle, you never have to toot it. Dogs cue on symbols. The sight of the whistle is more important than the blowing of it. Same with the flyswatter. Produce it, and the whole dog family will go flat, sheepishly concerned.

This is training with your head, not your hand. The flyswatter is not an instrument of brutality, it is a symbol immediately cued on, the same way as a motorist coming upon a red traffic light.

Training Ten Dogs

That's another reason it's simpler to train ten dogs than it is one. Not only do the dogs help you instill a technique such as the litter-box check cord, but they also share their emotions. Thus fear for one flushes over the whole house family. I get mad at one, and I've got five others walking on eggshells. But as I said before, command a dog by his name and the other dogs ignore what you're doing.

Just Say It Once

Now in all your association with Pup, don't be a nagger: The result will be a houseful of dogs with acid stomachs. Just give your command once and be done with it. That's why a voice that can blow bricks from a wall does have value. But you know, dogs hear well, remember? They're also sensing body odor, telepathy, and other subtle cues. So there's no need being a heavy unless you and Pup are in peril.

And as the dog matures, the loudness of your voice should lessen. I can now hiss something like "psssst," and swear it hasn't carried five feet—and dogs in the next room will come running to see what I'm upset about. If someone's talking quietly, don't you strain to listen? If another person is yelling, your impulse is to turn him off: Dogs are the same way. Whisper.

But there is a time to shout. You let Pup out the front door on a leash, but what's this? You drop the leash—and Pup bolts into the street after a cat. Well, Pup may be dead in two seconds if he's hit by a car. Therefore he must be stopped. When you yell "no!" I want Pup to stop as if he'd been shot through the brain.

SUMMARY

So let's conclude this chapter by saying this: If Pup will come when called and stop whatever he's doing when you say "no," then you've got the best-trained pup in the world. You don't need anything else.

But should you want advanced obedience, I'm going to give it to you. Pup don't need it. He'll learn to walk on a leash just by your snapping the thing to him, walking out the door, waiting for him to follow, then taking a step, seeing if he'll do the same. If not, put it all away and do it again the next night. Within three nights, Pup will heel anywhere in town.

He'll walk beside you, and when you stop, he'll stop. And when you start again, he'll start again. And you'll not say a word to him. I like that way of teaching much better than formally snapping Pup to a lead and meaning business as you order him through commands.

If you want something as adorable as this . . .

Make your training sessions deluxe time. Nothing tense or structured. Everything casual, and no one's in a hurry. For when we go to formal training, Pup is going to feel—for the first time—that you're becoming a heavy.

So remember—I'll repeat again—if Pup will come when called and stop when you say "no," you've got a fail-safe dog, and the best of all companions for life.

But you want more. Let's get it.

. . . you're going to have to put up with something as horrible-looking as this. (Remember what I told you about reading eyes? Take a look at these.)

11

Obedience Training

I was in Europe gathering gun-dog stories. In a Bavarian village a tall, thin man stood before me wearing a peaked hat. He told me, "This is Germany's national champion." I looked at the sitting German shorthaired pointer. The man then took the tractor-lug sole of his boot and ground the sitting dog's leg into the concrete street. "He must be tough," I was told, "so he can win."

Man's inhumanity against life will never end. This same German trainer also took me to a pond and produced a one-month-old dead duck. It was rank, featherless, absolutely hideous.

The man threw the duck into the pond and told the German shorthaired pointer to go fetch it. "If he doesn't," I was told, "I will beat him. He must never refuse to do anything I tell him."

Have you never before considered the plight of some dogs? So many of them have such bad lives, such beat-down lives. Sure there are a few ensconced on satin pillows faintly smelling of perfume. But the majority of dogs, if we think about them at all, are just tolerated—or ignored.

But working a dog humanely is not to deny him, rather, it is to exhilarate him. And in the hands of a thoughtful handler, a working dog can live the best of all canine lives.

Take the guide dog for the blind. Do you know there will never be one minute out of one day that this dog will not be on duty? Never to frolic in the sunshine, knock up chi-chi birds in the field, dive into the pond, or run with some child. But this guide dog is happy, contented, in love, bonded. You say, "The dog knows no difference." That's right, he doesn't. But that's not the point. We do. Man gets away with this twenty-four-hour-a-day canine servant because *dogs love to work.*

The service dog who gives life to the deaf and the paraplegic, who answers doorbells, and telephones, and opens the refrigerator door.

The shepherd on the wind-swept Highlands, ever vigilant, ever dutiful.

Do you know we have a dog called the goat dog? Know what he does? Well, the goat dog is usually some massive behemoth who is taken as a pup and placed with a herd of Texas mohair goats. He then, simply, becomes a goat. He's never named, never touched by human hands. A man comes sometime during each day and leaves food beside the desolate road. The dog leaves the goats long enough only to chow down.

And why is the goat dog there? Because he's going to flat execute any coyote that comes within a quarter of a mile of his beloved goat herd. (The dog has bonded!) "I dare you to attack a goat," is his motto. "I am a one-hundred-pound goat with canines, and I will kill you."

Do you know that an attack dog can never be a mean dog? That's right. He attacks with no more emotion than another dog who's told to sit. The attack dog is merely carrying out a command. For what would happen if the attack dog were mean? Well, a policeman returned to his K-9 car the other day to look in the window. He shuddered when he saw a three-year-old child sitting in the backseat with his attack dog. A mean dog could have killed the child for invading his territory. This trained dog merely sat beside the little girl, wagging his tail, panting happily.

So no dog ever resented being put to work: They're not like many humans I know, or read about these days.

But to everything there is an appointed season.

WHEN?

No ten-week-old pup ever successfully entered into a formal training program. It ain't possible.

Oh, you'll hear miracle stories. I hear them all the time. "My dog was responding to whistle and hand signals when he was six months old." Bosh.

It ain't what the dog's doing at six months that interests me. It's what he's doing at three years of age when he becomes mature and is now both capable and ready to fulfill a bona fide working dog's role.

And the reason I say this is that most six-month wonders are scuttled by the time they're a year old.

Oh, how many letters-to-the-editor I've received the past scores of years that said, "I don't know what's wrong with my pup. He won't come when called, he won't go fetch a ball, and he won't stay in one place while I walk around the block."

Well, ain't that fine? If the guy who's writing me says he's a plumber, I write back acknowledging that, naturally, his folks placed a pipe wrench in his hands when he was ten weeks old.

What's wrong, I charge, with letting these pups have their puppyhood? I sure enjoyed my childhood. And maybe you did, too. The enjoyment and the assurance that came with it certainly contributed to whatever joy I've had as an adult.

Same for dogs. Let them play and experiment and be lazy with their day or go flat insane digging a hole. Let them be what God put them on earth to be: pups.

Who gives a damn if the eight-week-old pup will heel, sit, stay?

I'm a dog trainer—that's my business—and I sure don't care. All I know is it's hurting the pup to try to teach him this stuff at an early age. For you give these prodigies a head start with some rapid-training method, and old plodder Tarrant will pass them about eighteen months of age with sensible training methods and never look back.

So never attempt to train a pup until he's ready to accept the lesson. Otherwise, you've got grudge and resentment and you may have just scuttled what could have been a good pup. *For you can take the spirit out of a pup, but you can't put it back in.* And nothing bad that ever happens to a pup can be associated with a human being.

Now, I've told you before and I'm going to remind you again, it's easier to train ten pups than it is one. Because pups (or dogs) train pups. You got a pup who won't give to the lead, which is required if he's to be taught heel, sit, stay. But you try to break him, and you'll end up with a sullen pup.

THE CHAIN GANG

But let a chain gang of dogs do it, and Pup will come to you giving to the lead and have nothing but good thoughts about you.

A chain gang? Yeah. For let's repeat: All dog training is based on point of contact, repetition, and association. And training any dog is like adding links to a chain. Link B fits in Link A, and Link C fits in Link B, and on down the length of the chain. If there's a weak link in training, you must stop, go back, and weld it shut. If not, you'll never know when Pup is going to "break."

Our point of contact is a wide, flat leather (or nylon) collar about Pup's neck that's outfitted with a welded D-ring. To this D-ring we attach the snap swivel connected to a drop-section hanging from a 22-foot length of steel chain.

Never, never, never use a choke collar made of chain, as recommended by most obedience experts. Such a collar can bruise or even crush Pup's trachea.

So imagine it's 1930 and it's wash day. You've got a chain stretched out on the ground instead of a clothesline in the air. Now every few feet there's a drop-chain attached to this long chain, which is staked to the ground by circus posts.

The 18-inch-long drop-chains are 66 inches apart, so no two dogs can touch each other and start a fight. Each drop-chain ends in a snap swivel.

Now here we come with Pup and snap the strong, welded D-ring on his leather or nylon collar to the drop-chain. Pup's had it.

For should you be lucky enough that your neighbors consent to your rounding up all the local dogs and snapping them to that chain, that chain is now going to rock, rattle, and roll.

And Pup is going to think the world has come to an end.

One dog will lunge and bark and snap. The chain will jerk forward and nearly snatch Pup off his haunches. Now another dog goes berserk. "You'll not treat me like this," he'll be screaming in dog talk, and Pup will be jerked this way, snapped back that way, knocked sideways.

The chain gang trains seven large dogs in one morning at the old farm.

Well, let's put it this way. After two hours of this you come back and all the pups have had it. They've dug trenches and now lie in the moist dirt of them, and if a garbage truck goes right through the backyard they'll probably not even alert.

Now you go in and rescue Pup. Do just that. Tell him, "What's the matter boy . . . these guys nuts? How did you get into such a fix, anyway? Well, come on now and let Daddy take care of you. Dog-gone, that's terrible. Let's go for a walk, okay?" And you take that lead in hand and heel Pup five miles, and he'll never jerk the line. Now, I call this dog training, do you?

Always use your head in training Pup, never your hand. Always situate Pup to self-train. If possible, let other dogs be your assistant pros. Always train with intimacy, never intimidation.

BASIC COMMANDS

Okay, let's heel, sit, stay.

Get a 22-foot nylon check cord, 5/8-inch in diameter (or a long, flat leash), and snap it to Pup's welded D-ring. Gather up all the surplus rope and carry it in a stack of loops like a cowboy hangs over his saddle horn.

Stand beside Pup and tell him, "Heel." Now, he don't know heel from hell, and couldn't care less. So you tap your outer leg—this gesture is very important for situating a dog at heel—and you keep arranging yourself and re-sitting Pup by tapping your leg, until the base of Pup's neck is immediately adjacent to the outside seam of your pants and he's looking the way you're standing. Hooray.

Now put some tension on the cord between your left hand and Pup's D-ring. Left hand? Yeah, most people are right-handed, so they usually heel Pup on the subordinate side.

Okay, got the tension? Now saying "heel," step off, keeping tension on the check cord. Pup may come, he may leap sideways, he may rear back, he may sit, he may bound straight in the air and fishtail.

Whatever he does, don't make an issue of it. If you had a chain gang of dogs, all this resistance to the lead would have been vented on his own kind.

If Pup's just not going to do it, then put it all away. Pup may live fifteen years; you sure don't need to get the job done tonight.

But let's say he comes along, staying to your side, not lunging, not falling back, not jerking out sideways, not crowding your knee. Fine. Keep walking. Now you want to stop, so do it gradually, let Pup sense you're slowing down. Now say "heel" again and flat stop. If Pup goes on, just hold the leash, et cetera.

When Pup has stopped moving—he's settled beside you—then praise him, I mean lay it on thick. Now start it all over again. Stepping out, stopping, until Pup's had enough.

Please remember: A pup's attention span is very short. No training session should ever be more than fifteen minutes. Read your dog; he'll show you how he's doing. When his head droops and his tail goes down, he's finished.

Also, this is one time another dog can't help you. Just the opposite. Have Pup in the field alone. No other dog or person can be there to distract him. Listen. The passing motorcycle can knock Pup off his game. Keep attentive.

Repeat your drill every other day for two weeks. Now you'll have a pup heeling.

SIT

It's time to teach Pup to sit. Just tell him to heel and have him locate at your side. Remember that I said to pat your outer leg to get Pup situated? Well, there's something else you can do: Make a circle with your hand while clicking your fingers.

Put your flat palm against Pup's nose then take your hand out and sweep it in a great circle away out and back to you. Pup will follow your clicking fingers—his nose will follow. He will make a complete turn beside you and come back to heel. Let's hope this time he's squared away with the world.

Now tell Pup, "Sit"—as you switch the lead to your right hand and holding it high, reach down with your left hand, making a span of your thumb and forefinger to press down immediately in front of Pup's hips. Pull up on Pup's collar with your right hand and push down on his hips with your left hand. Pup will sit.

Now tell him to heel and step forward. Two or three steps later, tell him to sit. And on and on and on. If Pup sits crooked, then re-seat him.

Now, I've got ten tons of tricks. And I'm not telling you all of them because *I don't want Pup hurt.* But here's one for you to do real easy, okay? If Pup's sitting but crowding your leg, which means the dog is asserting himself, then take your right foot, lift it, swing it softly behind your left leg, and catch Pup on the butt. Don't think he'll not wonder where that came from. This will startle him and he'll swing his rump away from you. But remember: I didn't say to kick him!

COME

When Pup's sitting, we can teach him to come. Place your hand before him, palm flat. Make an issue of it. Display the hand, moving it menacingly, and keep saying "sit" or "stay."

Now do an about-face and step off backward. Pup will probably want to follow. No, he can't. You are abrupt in your voice, even harsh, saying, "No, no, no, no!" Only now you are in front of Pup, so you're holding up your flat palm as a traffic cop would display at an intersection.

Now try to back away. Keep facing Pup and walk backward. Hold the 22-foot check cord in your hands. Keep backing up, telling him, "Stay." If Pup starts to move then stop him with raised palm and harsh voice.

You can also stand beside Pup and throw the check cord out before the two of you. Then you back out with nothing in your hands. Upon reaching the end of the cord, you reach down, grasp it, and, saying "come," you milk Pup in.

Or with cord in hand, when you are twenty feet away, rest for a moment, then say, "Come," to Pup, and milk the cord, hand-over-hand, or hold the cord lightly in your left hand and milk it through with your right hand. Pup'll run to you.

So now you've taught heel, sit, stay, and come.

And mind you, I've said nothing of it, but you know Pup's responding to the whole gestalt of you—touch, smell, feel, hearing—FIDO. He's noting your facial expression, your posture, the heat of your aura. All we've discussed up front is happening, is going on, between you and Pup. That's what's training him. Not the rope and collar. It's you. The tools are secondary.

Always remember Joe Simpson's land-mine dogs. Were those dogs reacting to scent or to ESP? We don't know now and maybe never will. But be aware of both possibilities and know this: Pup's reacting to the whole essence of you. Be his thoughtful helper and be kind.

Also, should you want Pup to learn the command "down," when you've milked him into you on the command "come," then tell him, "Sit," and bend over, pull out his front feet and let his body ease to the earth as you say, "Down." Or make a pulley of the space between your shoe heel and sole, thread your leash through the gap, and, as you push down with your left hand, pull up the leash with your right hand.

A Grounding Stick

But let's say Pup won't stay as you back away. Then we'll fix it so he can't move.

Cut a piece of a broomstick the distance from your solar plexus to your groin. (This is the correct length for dogs the size of German shepherds, Labrador retrievers, and dalmatians. For smaller dogs, measure the distance from their collar to the ground and cut the broomstick twice as long. But remember, small dogs are feisty. They can leap to the side quickly, and the wedged stick may prove useless.) Drill a hole in each end. Tie (or snap) one end of the broomstick to Pup's welded D-ring. Tie the other end of the broomstick to your check cord.

Now hold the stick in your left hand as you stand beside Pup and keep telling him, "Heel."

But what's this? Suddenly you toss your end of the stick out to the front so it wedges into the ground—angling back up to Pup's D-ring—as the check cord continues to sail out to the front. Now you do an about-face in front of Pup and walk backward, leaving Pup behind. Should he try to move, he'll just walk into the wedge of the stick. The stick will push against the D-ring, and the other end will dig into the earth before Pup. Pup can't step forward. Hooray. Now we've got him.

Once you've reached the end of your rope—some twenty feet away—then cheerily tell Pup to "come," as you flip your check cord and lift the angled stick from the ground. Milk the cord fast so the stick won't hit the ground as Pup races toward you. Now it's guaranteed you'll successfully teach Pup to stay.

When all this is down pat, then about-face before Pup with the tension of the cord keeping the stick parallel to the earth. Start backing away, keeping tension on the check cord to keep the stick high and parallel to the ground. Tell Pup to stay.

If he doesn't offer to move forward, you can back up to your length of twenty-two feet. But if he should start to move—and you can read this—then merely release the tension on the cord. The stick will drop and wedge, and Pup will be held fast.

You must learn to read Pup. And you will. But the fiftieth pup you train will be much easier to figure—to read—than your first.

Take the case of Pup sitting and starting to move forward. Focus on his shoulder muscles, his upper front legs. You know the muscles there have to twitch (or roll) before Pup can lift a paw. So you're always reading signs far ahead of Pup actually breaking your command.

Mike Gould, with miracle dog Web, shows how to press a grounding stick to reinforce staying.

Mike lifts the grounding stick and tells Web: "Come here."

PENNIES

You'll note the only training aids I've asked you to assemble are a fly-swatter, a dog whistle, a collar, a rope, and a broomstick. Honest, folks, you don't have to spend a lot of money to train a pup. What's important ain't equipment, it's you.

Except for possible vet bills, a dog is not expensive. And when I had all my big working dogs, I never went to the vet, unless there was a fight. Big dogs, living in the outdoors, just seldom get sick.

But house dogs? That's another matter.

Still it costs nothing to train either type.

DON'T KILL PUP

In training Pup to heel, sit, stay, and come, there's one thing we didn't do. We didn't use food—a commercially processed tidbit—as

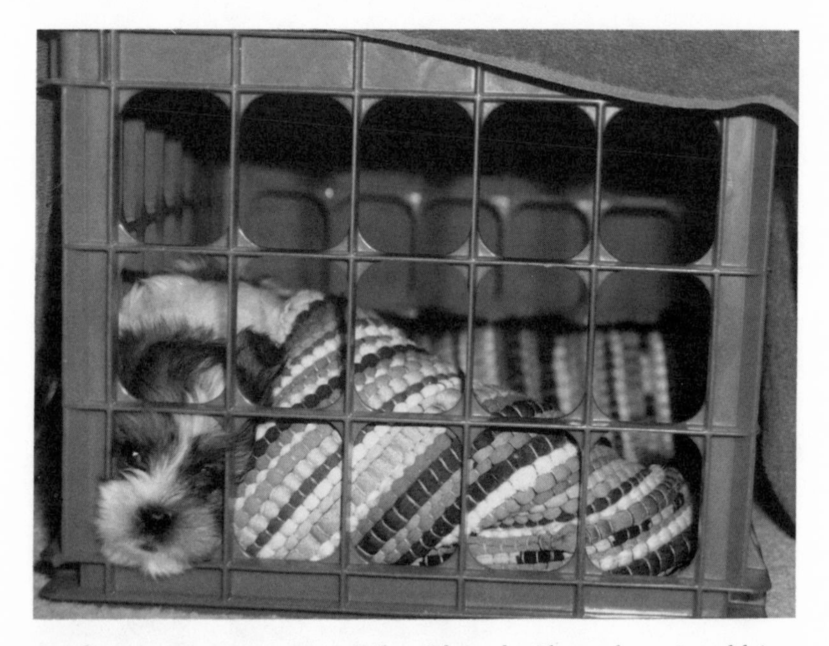

It takes pennies to raise a pup. When I brought Champ home I couldn't find the airline kennel so I put him in a milk crate.

a lure. Anybody can offer Pup the smell of a "treat" then back away, saying, "Come," and Pup will surely do just that.

Food is of importance to a dog second only to a human's love. And there are times that the two seem to be a tie. Dogs flat love to eat.

But know this: While you're trying to train Pup with treats, you may be killing him.

Due to unique dog experiences in my life, I'm convinced that too much protein is a primary killer of man's best friend. Check those commercially prepared tidbits: Do they not say 15 percent, 17 percent, 22 percent, or more of *minimum* protein. Well, protein in these quantities—in excess of a dog's daily meal(s)—for a partially sedentary dog may hurt his kidneys. And when the kidneys go, so goes the dog.

So don't try to educate Pup by killing him.

There will be a lot of attention paid to this in our chapter on nutrition. But for now, try to follow my suggestions and get Pup to comply with all requests without bribing him with food. And for the same reason, don't feed Pup table scraps, either.

The Value of Obedience

Oh, yes, I almost forgot. Remember I told you it was possible to bring a pup along without training. I did it with the twin Lhasas. But Mike Gould, with the miracle dog Web, tells me, "Whenever Web gets sloppy on the hidden elastic rubber band—like he doesn't move the right direction, stuff like that—then I bring him in, run him through a set of basic obedience drills, and then when I send him out, he's perfect again."

Therefore, obedience does have great value. I don't say it doesn't. I'm just so frightened that too many people, when they teach obedience, will get frustrated and hurt Pup. I'd rather they didn't try to teach him at all if that's to be the consequence.

QUIET

Remember my telling you the late Er Shelley of Columbus, Mississippi, was the greatest dog trainer who ever lived? As a teenager living with his parents in their Michigan hotel, Er wanted a pack of dogs but his dad told him he would have to keep them quiet. No disturbing the guests' sleep. So Er housed them in the backyard and monitored them from his second-story bedroom. Whenever they barked, Er whispered to them to shut up. They did. That's how heavy-voiced you need to be as a dog trainer.

And this, too. I've given you standard commands. But everyone has their own way of saying things. If I enter a door and all the dogs are jammed there, I say, "Scoot." Throughout the day, I'm saying, "Okay," which tells the dogs I'm moving and to give me a path, or that I'm going outdoors so they can tinkle and dump. Whenever I see errant behavior, I no longer yell, "No," or the dog's name, or whatever. I say, "Psssst." It works. And it's nearly silent. But when I get fed up with the barking—and I do—I bellow, "Hey!" And that works, too.

Use what you like. Say "Niagara Falls," if it pleases you, to have Pup roll over. In England the command for "down" is "charge." Get the scene: You have a rottweiler, your friend is naturally scared, you put on a grim face and yell, "Charge," and the friend knows his life has ended—only to see the great rottweiler sink to earth like a deflated balloon. Have fun.

12

Putting Pup Through College

This is an old story but it bears retelling here. Sometimes it doesn't pay to put a dog through advanced training. A duck hunter wanted to show off his Lab, so he took a guest hunting. The hunter cast the Lab for a duck, and the dog ran across the water. The hunter said, "Ain't that a miracle?" And the guest said, "Sure is . . . that dog can't swim."

There's a ton of stuff you can teach Pup if you want to. You know how I feel about it: I'd prefer the dog to self-train. But I want to help you and Pup every way I can so let's see how we can get a few odd jobs done.

The Leaping Pup

Sure 'nuf some gal will come through the door, and Pup will leap and rip her nylons. The gal's mad, the pup's repentant, and you're flabbergasted. "He never did that before," you have to say. That sort of thing.

Well, there are ways to stop Pup from leaping, and they all involve force. See why I don't like advanced training? But you and I will figure out a way to do it where our force is no more than an angel's kiss.

When Pup's rearing up—you can read him, you know when he's

going to jump (remember FIDO). For you see the coiled pelvic drive muscles, and you read the gleam in Pup's eyes.

Besides, you know the occasions when he'll jump, like when you return home. Or in this instance, when a stranger comes through the door. So be ready.

As Pup comes up, lift your knee and bump him in the chest. Easy does it. You can literally send him sailing backward to splat flat on his back with too much force.

So what happens? Pup learns fast. But not what you want to teach. So now he leaps up the side of your leg, and your knee can't bend to knock him away.

So what to do now?

You can take Pup's paw in hand and squeeze it. He'll yipe and jump down. Or you can reach out with your shoe and step on Pup's toes. See, I told you I didn't like any of it, but I agreed to show you.

So those are some of the professional trainer's ways. But how about just talking to Pup, letting him know you don't want him up on you. That works. But it takes some time.

So let's say we've stopped Pup from leaping on us. But a stranger enters the house, and up he goes.

So we get an accomplice to enter the house. Pros do this all the time: They bring in a ringer. Your co-worker at the plant agrees to help you, and in he comes and what's this: His knee comes up, too, and Pup goes sailing. Now Pup's going to reassess all this jumping. It hurts. He doesn't want any more of it. Everybody's got a trick knee.

But mind this: While you are catching Pup with your knee and sending him back from you, don't show any expression in your face. Pup'll see it and know you meant it. Be neutral. Like nothing happened. *Always be this way whenever Pup must be touched in training.* For you'll recall our definition of communication: that which is shared equally by two or more. Pup will share whatever feeling you have when you bump him: Don't feel malice, or he'll sense it. And the consequence will be you've alienated a pup who otherwise was coming along well.

But Sandy Burns, a veteran working-dog enthusiast who trains obedience dogs, cart dogs, herding dogs, and therapy dogs, comes to our rescue. She says, "If a dog's sitting, then he can't jump. So teach sit so that it sticks." And she's right. But the dog's got to be foolproof. I mean, you've really got to put in a heavy-duty sit. And it can be done. Before a guest enters the house, command, "Sit." This really puts pressure on the dog—but it is ultimate dog training. Also, you have much more body movement to read: It takes more motion to jump from sit than it does from standing. So you read the dog (FIDO) and command him to stay before he can jump.

The Total Calamity

There's no bedlam like a dogfight. It's as chaotic, frantic, and bewildering as a year-end-closeout Toyota TV commercial. And if the dogs are large and tenacious, you'll have a hell of a time getting them apart. So this is exactly what you must do.

Remember Moby, the leviathan Pyrenees at the farm? Well, he patrolled the place so he established territory. But Scoop was a huge Lab who had other ideas. Yet Scoop was kenneled with all the other Labs.

So each night when we would all walk around the pond, here would come Moby to stand by as I opened Scoop's gate. Usually there would be a display, nothing more. But one night lightning struck. The result: I drove Scoop into town to the vet, and as he worked on Scoop, he told me, "It takes me maybe five minutes to pull one of these canine teeth, and that big white dog did it in a half-second."

There is nothing so totally calamitous as a dogfight. And if you've got big dogs, then too often they must fight to the end. For there's nothing you can do.

Two tips: Hit both dogs with a high-pressure water hose. But how are you going to do that if your dog is attacked as you walk down the street?

So here's where we spray the attacking dog with cayenne pepper. You can buy these pepper sprayers at most flea markets. That's sure going to stop the fight. But remember: The sprayed dog is going to go nuts with inflamed eyes. He'll run and scoot and cry and cavort. And if you flush his eyes with water, it just makes the pepper hotter. And the effect lasts forty-five minutes. So what's the answer? I have none. It is imperative we break up the fight, and the two antagonists will just have to pay the price.

But with small dogs, the best thing to do is for two people, each grabbing a dog by his hind legs, to pull the dogs apart and swing each of them in great circles. For a dog, that's total disarmament. For you see, man, dog, or horse, take away their legs and they're yours.

Now monitor the dogs. If they're still growling and their necks are bent with jaws down and they're looking fiercely for the opponent, then swing them again. Never put their feet to earth unless they've cooled down. Otherwise, I can predict the fight will erupt again.

Now I'm going to tell you why these dogfights are so serious. One dog can kill another—that's serious enough. But they are certain to injure each other to some degree. And many a would-be peacemaker has been bitten severely. So watch yourself.

Now, listen. There aren't many wounds more serious than a puncture wound, or a dog bite. When a dog opens his mouth and bites, he makes a puncture wound with his upper jaw, plus a puncture wound with his lower jaw. When he closes his mouth, he tears the tissue from top to bottom where he's biting. The result? The dog bite has loosened all that skin from the top of the wound to the bottom, and four or five days later, you'll get a big abscess there. And if you get a gas-producing gangrene, the dog can even die. So vet care is obligatory.

Once again we have a truth that is immutable. A fighting pup will become a fighting dog. They never quit. Not in a lifetime. Not even if beaten severely. There's just some maniacal drive in them to attack and sustain it. You'll never rid them of it.

Simulated Sex

Most dogs have a latent urge for sex even if they're immature, spayed, or neutered. No matter how hard you try to be blasé, still it will embarrass you when Pup decides to mount his housemate in front of company. Or try to mount the company itself. So when no one else is present, display the flyswatter as you bark Pup's name, and he will quit. Then, when company's present, merely calling Pup's name will put him down. If not, keep the flyswatter tucked between the sofa cushions and display it. Pup will walk away. Of course, we go back to Sandy Burns. If you tell the dog to sit, he's got to dismount to comply. That's a test.

In the long run, repeated mountings by Pup can be brought to an end by the dog he's covering. The bottom dog seldom cares for this and will let the top dog know it.

Keep Off the Furniture

Now there's an electrical device on the market that will shock a dog who leaps on your sofa. Another will emit an ultrasonic whistle that will drive Pup away. As for me, I don't care. Pup's welcome to it. But you may think differently and it's your dog I'm training. And it's your furniture Pup's lounging on.

Well, shock them if you want to: I wouldn't think of it.

Hit them with the whistle; that's not injurious.

Also, you can drive the dog from your furniture when you actually see him transgress. And you can tell him to never, never get up there again. Good luck.

As for me, if I were concerned about my sofa, I'd put a cover over it: a blanket or something. Then let the dog have it. When snooty company comes, I'd uncover the thing and let the interlopers have it. Only trouble there is that the dogs will fight them for space. It was their sofa before these strangers came.

That's where so many dog owners fail. They won't train their dogs before the fact. They let the dogs jump on them. Then, when a stranger visits, they get terribly upset because the dog wants to jump on this newcomer. Doesn't make any sense, does it? Think ahead and train ahead.

TEACHING ROVER TO JUMP

Sometimes it's necessary that Pup jump: He sure has to when getting in the back of a station wagon. So let's teach him how.

This is easy, folks. Just put Pup in one room and you get in the other. Place a piece of one-by-four wood upright on the floor across the door, and Pup will jump it.

Then keep building your obstacle higher until Pup's jumping a card table you've propped up there. Nothing to it, is there?

And I repeat: The order to jump and enter any enclosed space is "kennel."

There's something else I do with this kennel thing that you should try. If you want Pup to move into an enclosed space, or into another room, or another part of the yard, then teach him to do it this way.

Leave the lighted utility room and go into the darkened garage. Stay with Pup, or leave him there. Go back later to open the door to the lighted room and tell Pup, "Kennel." He'll probably jump at the chance; if he's a young pup, the blackened garage may prove spooky.

I also do this with my car. I arrive home after taking Pup for a ride, and he won't get out. So I leave him there—take your car keys with you so Pup doesn't accidentally lock the car doors with the keys inside—and go into the house. Later when I return, I tell Pup, "Come here," and he's mighty happy to leap into my arms.

Snapping

Some dogs get so excited that they snap at you when you hand out a treat. Don't put up with it. Stop it quickly. The way to do this is very simple. Hold a treat in your closed fist. Present the fist to Pup. He'll sniff but not snap. Then turn your hand over before his face and open your fingers slowly. Angle your hand down, and Pup has no fingers to catch. Instead, he will lap the treat out of your open palm with his tongue or lips.

Then test Pup. Hold out a treat. If he starts to snap, then jerk the tidbit away, saying, "No," and put on Momma-dog's frown. You know Momma-dog, she's all mock malice, great guttural issue, slitted eyes, bowed neck. Imitate that. Pup will decipher it. Just don't ever let Pup snap again, or folks, this can get bad and you'll have many bit fingers. That may not be so bad for you, but what about the visiting child who unwittingly holds out her pacifier, and Pup almost takes her hand off grabbing what he assumed was a treat?

The other night, Tiffy and Candy had a go at it, and Dee reached in—only to get her thumb crushed. The nail was blue for a week, and she complained often that it really hurt. A dog bite is real.

Chasing Cars

I know your pup's not going to chase cars: that would mean you didn't love him, for you let him run loose.

But the neighbor's dog may jump you as you pull away, and the dog's so aggressive you know he's going to get run over and you don't want to get sued.

Okay, let the car-chasing pup get to running in full force and come right up alongside, whereupon you have an accomplice in the backseat dump a whole bucket of water on him. That'll do it. Dogs usually hate sprayed or dumped water.

Or same principle: Let the guy in the backseat reach out and really give Pup a snootful of cayenne pepper. That'll do it, too.

DIGGING IN THE YARD

If you want to meet a dog trainer who's been defeated by digging pups, then say hello to me.

Digging, like fighting, is just inborn in some pups. And folks, you'll have a hell of a time getting it out of them. And the real problem is that if you've got one digger in the house, he'll teach the same to every new pup.

I've bought those portable show-ring fences. (You may want one. They make a wide circle or an extended fence and collapse down to a flat of panels.) So what? The dogs just dig someplace I haven't fenced in. I've also bought small flower-bed panels to keep the dogs out—and they jump over them.

So there's only one way to go. Spray everywhere the dogs dig with cayenne pepper each day. (For young pups, use Bitter Apple.) Finally the dogs will run out of places to dig and give it up.

However, if you are actually keeping your dog in an outside pen because you have no alternative, then extend your chicken-wire or hog-wire paneling down into the earth. So when Pup digs, he continually hits a wire barrier and never escapes.

You can also pour your kennel run with concrete and stop the digging, but dogs on concrete get splatted feet. Put heavy-duty gravel in there, and the dog will stand all day tensing his paws and keeping a tight foot. This is an asset for a field dog who must run.

BARKING

We've spoken of this problem up front and decided a Barker Breaker (that's the name of a manufactured product) is our best tool. Here's how it works. The dog barks. The breaker emits a high-pitched sound. The dog is startled and shuts up.

But there are other ways.

For kennel-kept dogs, run plumbing above each run. Water is controlled by a valve attached to a solenoid that will trigger on sound and release a shower. Dogs hate sprayed water. A Lab can spend his whole day swimming in a lake, but spray him with water, and he'll act like you doused him with acid.

Or you can tie a bunch of tin cans together and rig the rope so it goes to your bedroom window. When the dog barks, open the window, release the rope, and drop the cans on the concrete. There'll not be a dog in sight. They'll all be scrunched up in the backs of their houses.

Or if you have house dogs, just keep the white flyswatter by the back door. Tell the dogs to shut up, show them the swatter, and you'll have a quiet yard.

BOLTING

We don't want Pup killed. I took the gang to the groomer in Sedona and opened the back of the wagon and Tiffany (one year old) leaped and ran. There was no way I could catch her with my stoved-up legs. She ran to a junkyard and had a circus flashing from one discarded car body to another. Then into a car mechanic's garage. Whee, what fun. Now into an industrial-glass warehouse. Then down the road to her possible death.

The woman groomer appeared and offered to help. Tiffy was whelped by a twenty-year-old woman. The groomer called and Tiffy immediately ran to her. After one year there was still that strong female association. The woman picked Tiffy up and carried her into the building. I sat on the tailgate of the wagon and told myself I was a damned poor trainer. Why had I never taught the pups to heel, sit, stay? Because they were an experiment. I wanted to see what two totally unfettered pups would do. Well, I found out, right?

But I could have controlled that bolt of Tiffany's so easily. All I had to do was take along a spray bottle of water and when I opened the tailgate let her have it in the face. She would have retreated to the front of the car. Great trainer, huh? After the fact.

So the way to stop bolting is to teach a rock-hard heel, sit, stay.

Then when you open the wagon gate, give those commands, get the dogs sitting—*then* spring the latch.

At home your dogs will naturally rush the front door when the doorbell rings. Once again, it's heel, sit, stay. But something else that's effective is to have a friend ring the doorbell. The dogs will bolt to the opened door. Only your friend has the flyswatter, and he yells and waves it and the whole house pack ducks back inside. They'll not try that again.

PUP KEEPS PESTERING YOU

There's a simple thing you can teach that really helps. Many times a dog will sit beside your chair at the table and beg for your food Or he will push his dish about, asking (in his own way) for more. Or you give one treat, and look to see Pup standing up, begging, and not accepting no for an answer.

So here's where we teach the command "no more." That's it. Just

Dee displays her empty hands and tells her beggars: "It's all gone."

say "no more," and bare your hands before Pup's face. Lower your palms, face out, and tell Pup in a disappointed voice, "No more."

It's uncanny how fast Pup will pick up on this. And I know of no other command more effective. Just say, "No more," show your palms, and Pup will turn and walk away. Honest.

THE PROBLEM WE CAN'T THINK OF

You'll have other problems to solve for yourself. Just remember: communication. No matter what you are doing, somehow, some way, you are transmitting to Pup all the time. And if you're ignoring him, you're not sensing his feedback.

You'll have no friend like the white flyswatter. It is a symbol, you know. It represents the sternest you. Pup sees that swatter and even in your absence he smells you, sees you, feels you, senses you. The swatter represents all those no-nonsense things you become when Pup displeases you. The swatter is power. Just display it, call out Pup's name, and he will shrivel, tuck his tail, duck, and walk sideways from the room. Never forget your flyswatter. It is the ultimate problem solver.

EASY DOES IT

Whatever the problem, approach it with your head, not your hand. Use intimacy instead of intimidation. Help Pup through his ordeal; don't beat him through it.

And really, folks, if you can just hold out, all Pup's problems will eventually self-solve. Take Muffy: She's dying, yet her sense of duty is beyond reality. She can't control her bladder all that well, but she'll make it to the yard before she releases every time. I never saw such a sense of dedication. And Muffy was a hellion when we brought her home.

I put a collar on her; she screamed until I took it off. I put her within a portable pen on the grass in the backyard. She reared and ran and leaped until I let her out.

She tinkled on the floor that night and I picked her up and surprised her. She bit me.

So, see, it will work out for the best. Have patience and remember: You couldn't walk for ten months. How long did it take to potty-train you? It took me five years to learn how to tie my shoes.

All in all, Pup will probably cause you less trouble than you caused your folks. Be kind.

13

The Routine

Two Arkansas boys were stealing hogs. The sheriff waited for them at a bridge. But the boys went him one better and dressed the stolen hog in a frock and bonnet and scrunched it up between them in the truck seat. The sheriff waved the boys down and approached the truck. He searched to find nothing and finally asked who the girl was. The boys told him she was Ima Hog and drove on. When they disappeared from sight the sheriff told his deputy, "Well, they ain't stealing hogs but they better stop drinkin'. That Ima Hog is the ugliest gal I ever saw."

There's nothing a dog likes more than going for a ride. I pile them all in the car—except for the upchuckers—and away we go each night. We drive around the block with their heads hanging out the windows. They bark at what interests them, and people in their yards stare in wonder. When we get home, the pack is rejuvenated and ready for another day. Nothing picks a dog up like a ride around the block.

When we got to Sedona, Muffy looked as though she'd die that night. The next three days she sought refuge on the bed, her eyes opaque and lifeless, her body limp. Then Dee suggested over the telephone (Dee was on the road) that I take Muffy for a ride, and I did. The next day Muffy left the bed, begged for food, and came down to the first floor to help me work. A ride can work miracles.

But know this! The most mellow, mild-mannered dog can become a vicious assailant if he establishes territory in your car. Never, never, never stick your fingers through a slit in some car window to touch a cute little fluff. That scruffy little doo-dad dog could well become unraveled and sail as a missile with dental warhead completely across that car and onto your hand.

Watch your own dog as well. Bill Berlat, my Tucson attorney buddy, and I were turkey hunting in northern Arizona. We had Gunner, a one-hundred-pound Chesapeake Bay retriever along for the ride. Gunner was always a little hyper but on this trip he seemed to settle down.

We stopped for a bucket of chicken at Kentucky Fried Chicken and as the girl handed it out, a woolly, copper-colored jughead slashed over Berlat's left shoulder and a chilling, ominous snap just missed the girl's wrist.

Always watch your dog in a car. You never know when he will attack someone passing by.

And as for those upchuckers . . . hope springs eternal, right? Just get something from the vet and Pup can go. But it doesn't work that way. My experience with Dramamine, Benadryl, or whatever—the dog still gets sick from motion sickness. Other people may have had better luck than I, but no prescription has helped one of my upchucking dogs.

And I'll add fast: Those big dogs I hauled on the field-trial circuit, and the collies, and all the rest. Never a problem. They could ride to Mars and never get nauseated. But many little dogs just can't take it.

CHOW HOUNDS

Dogs love to eat. What else is so important?

For years I fed one time a day. No more. I now feel twenty-four hours is too long to go without something in their stomachs. So they get split rations. I now split into two feedings the amount I used to feed one time a day.

I'm still not going to talk about nutrition—that deserves its own chapter—but I want you to do this:

1. Feed each dog in the same place every time. Never deviate. If they're off their food the location, itself, will trigger them. Remember what I told you about dogs associating place with events. And having a specific place to go each time keeps down dogfights. Yes, dogs will fight over food.

2. Always feed the same diet. If you're going to change foods, then do it by mixing the old and new foods together for at least a week. Otherwise your dog may get diarrhea.

3. Place the food dish on a place mat or towel to keep the floor or carpet clean.

4. Avoid plastic dishes, for there is such a thing as plastic dermatitis, which is a horrible skin inflammation on a dog's face. After years of testing food plates, I found the best to be those by Rubbermaid: There's a number 3838 on the back.

Of equal value is Corning's Corelle dinnerware. Corelle is breakable, but yesterday I fed Sugar on a window seat so the twins wouldn't bother her, and when finished she gave her plate a toss and it clanged off the stone fireplace—didn't break.

These plates are great for so many reasons. They last forever, they are dishwasher safe, can go into the fridge, and are perfect in the microwave. Incidentally, when you store a can of dog food with a plastic lid and remove it to heat—put the food on a Rubbermaid plate and set the microwave for a range of forty seconds at the 4 temperature setting, or sixty seconds with a setting of 6 (depending on the microwave's KW). Any hotter than this, or longer than this, and the meat stinks. Also, by leaving a Rubbermaid plate in the microwave over ninety seconds at full power, I've had the bottom flake off.

There are many ways you can dispense kibbles. Most bowls will do. And I used to self-feed. You know, the dog stuck his head through a flap and by gravity flow the food fell down so the dog could eat what he wanted. It was great for field dogs who worked every day, but not for house dogs. You must really monitor the intake of house dogs because they are not active enough to burn up large amounts of calories.

Keep fresh water available at all times, and make sure it's bottled water if your city's water has too many hard chemicals for Pup's system.

A PLACE TO SLEEP

There are all kinds of sleeping arrangements available for Pup. Small dogs in the winter may need a sweater. I don't care if the critics think you're being fashion-conscious or not.

Mail-order houses offer all kinds of beds. One that's great is filled with cedar shavings. But never, never permit a dog to sleep on wheat straw. It can make him sick.

I really feel sorry for the outdoor dog now. When I had outdoor dogs, I had specially designed houses with hallways and an inner room to help my dogs keep either warm or cool—depending on the season. The houses were special in having a slant roof I could raise to look inside and do things like change bedding. A bitch with pups could jump onto the roof to evade her brood for a moment. Or a dog could get up there to sun in the winter or take the breeze in the summer.

But still, I've never found an outdoor doghouse that was adequate. That didn't have drafts, that didn't somehow leak or take in wind-blown mists. How great it would be if all dogs could stay inside.

If I hadn't got arthritis and was still training and running the big dogs, I'd have a screened lightbulb in there for each of the dogs to keep warm and cozy.

TRAVELING CROSS-COUNTRY

Traveling cross-country used to be fun. The Labs and I would load up in the spring and come back in the fall, making the big field-trial circuit from Texas to Montana. But those were better days than we have now. There was less traffic, people were more accommodating, and access was easier. I used to let the dogs out in a schoolyard to air. There was usually a tall fence there, and it would help me keep them all together. We'd water, feed, and stretch, and I'd talk to the kids who came over and wondered if I were with the circus.

Now we have those designated rest areas. Don't you know every dog in the world has been obligated to use that same little patch of dirt beside the interstate? And parvo, for example, is spread by air. So my dogs are out there kicking back that dust in a high wind. No way.

I once stopped at a major motel that advertised it had facilities for dogs. What a mess. A barrel out back in a scraped dirt prison yard. However, I will tell you this. Probably the best kennel facilities on a commercial property I've seen are at Disneyland. There is no way I can fault what I saw—and smelled—there. And, to be fair, I must tell you there is a booklet that lists all motels in North America that accept pets. And some of these inns—maybe most of them—are bound to be good. I've never tried them out, but I figure you could give them a try. (Ask any motel chain where you can get this booklet.)

So make the best of it when you travel with Pup. Ignore those signs that say dogs must be let out only here. I don't want my dog dead. I'll let them out where it's best for them, not best for the state.

One time I had all my dogs loose in a big city park, and a policeman approached me, saying, "You know you're breaking our city ordinance."

"How's that?" I asked.

"It says you must have your dog on a leash at all times."

I told him, "I'll bet it doesn't. I'll bet it says your dog must be under control at all times."

"Same thing," muttered the policeman.

"No it isn't," I told him. "Watch this." I heeled a Lab, told him to line, and cast him in a nonswerving race a city block long across that mowed lawn. Then I whistled him down, gave a hand cast to the right, let him run several yards, and hit him with the whistle again. Then I gave the suck-in whistle and brought him back to heel.

I turned to the cop and said, "Nobody ever had a leash that long . . . and that dog was under control all the time."

The man gave me a sheepish grin.

So I eased up when I told him, "You better have your city fathers write that ordinance again."

He got in his car and left, wishing me a good trip down the road. I wished him the same.

But there's a moral to this story: As far as hogs and dogs are concerned, the law doesn't always catch all the nuances.

To me dogs are first-class citizens. Tell me, who do you let live in your house, eat at your table, and sleep in your bed? And dogs pay taxes, too. What do you think that dog tag is? So, I'll sneak them into the motel. Let them swim in the golf-course pond. Walk them in the park. Look for any sanitary place for them to air. And use it!

THE BABY-SITTER

We don't always take Pup with us on vacation. Take him to Hawaii, for example, and he'd have to fly in the belly of the plane, plus spend his entire vacation in quarantine.

So who are you going to get to pet-sit? I'm telling you this can really be a big problem. For what you want is someone who's been around dogs. Don't matter if they are reliable, clean, concerned, and all that good stuff. If they don't have a history of handling dogs, you can be asking for lots of trouble.

So I always insist that my dog-sitters come from either the Humane Society or a vet clinic. These people handle dogs every day. They know what to expect, have skill in canine management, and know, as well, what to look for in the way of illness or depression—and what to do about it.

I pay well because I want these same people back year after year. My last sitter was with us eight years, and then I lost her to Montana, where she said she could breathe. Don't blame her. And, oh yes, when I met her, she was a volunteer at the Humane Society.

Now, some sitters want you to bring the dog to their homes. No way. Most homes are too hectic. And there are too many doors that can be left open, too many holes in the fence, and so forth. You know your property is fail-safe; you don't know about theirs. And who is in that sitter's home? A drunk, maybe, who might kick Pup in the ribs? Always insist Pup stays home.

THE BOARDING KENNEL

But what if you can't find anyone to care for Pup at home? Then you're going to have to use the services of a commercial boarding kennel. And regarding these institutions, folks, I've seen the worst and best of them.

There's a boarding kennel in Sedona called Bark and Purr. There was a time we kenneled the twin westies Punk and Tug there. We'd pull up in the car, the kids would see that building, and they would go nuts trying to scratch their way out. When released they would run to the door and paw to get in. There was just something about that place these dogs craved, and I'll trust my dog's judgment as to what's best anytime.

Jim Charlton of Sauvie Island, up in Portland, Oregon—remember him, he thought real hard and the dog named Casey came to him—runs a superlative boarding facility. Jim tells me the secret of a good boarding kennel is *no stress.* So each of his runs is floored, walled, and has a ceiling. There is a solid door the dog cannot see through. The place is well lighted, cool, and expertly painted. Beside each kennel door is a bouquet hanging in a pot. Listen and you'll hear piped-in music to soothe the nerves of the most upset beast.

On the hallway floor beside each door is that special little thing the owner brought to pacify Pup. After the kennel runs are cleaned, Pup can have his toy.

You should know this about dogs. Remember the song Bobby Goldsboro was singing in the early 1970s? It went: "If you can't be with the one you love, then love the one you're with." That's Pup. I don't care how well bonded he is. Dogs are opportunists, strategists, and master manipulators. The moment you are out of sight, they make a play for the kennel boy. Some boarding operators say they don't want you to bring anything that reminds Pup of you. They want him to give up all memory of the past and adjust to their regimen and domain. Makes sense.

What to Look For

There's a boarding kennel in Scottsdale, Arizona, that picks your pup up in a stretch limo and delivers him to a room—not a run—but a room with furniture, TV, music, the whole shebang. Well, I ain't paying for that, and you probably ain't either.

So what's next?

The average good boarding kennel has these features:

- it's clean
- it doesn't stink
- each dog has both an inside and outside run
- there are automatic water lickers so Pup has constant clean water
- the kennel operator feeds the diet you bring
- strange dogs are not kenneled together
- there are masonry walls between each kennel run, and they are high enough so a male dog can't spray his urine into the adjacent kennel
- the walls are also high so boarding dogs can't fence-fight
- there is music

- the boarding kennel has an ironclad and age-old arrangement with an "in-house" vet
- the kennel has high-pressure water (or steam) to wash down each kennel run and a trough to carry all refuse away to a sewer
- no other dog's feces or urine can run through your dog's kennel
- if your dog is going to be there any length of time, there must be kennel help to take Pup for a walk in an adjacent field
- which means the kennel must set on ample property
- at least once, and hopefully twice each week, each kennel run is sterilized
- Pup's bedding is picked up and stowed when the run is sluiced down
- bitches in heat are placed in isolation
- as well as any dog known to be ill
- there can be no part of the kennel run constructed of wood, for that soaks up water, harbors bacteria, and is too often chewed up and eaten by a bored pup
- the kennel floor is electrically heated, and, as a bonus, the place is equipped with automatic fire sprinklers
- the management doesn't lie
- if they don't ask you for Pup's vaccination record, then they're not very conscientious.

I checked a sick dog into a Phoenix boarding kennel that promised a country-club environment. The manager accepted my offer to pay extra for this old dog to stay in the main building—it was 110 degrees outside and the kennel runs were probably 185 degrees.

Well, when I got back, I had one emaciated pooch—she had been left out in the sun the whole time I was gone. My arthritis wasn't that bad in those days, but I held my temper. Otherwise I'd have thrown that guy into one of his kennel runs, locked the gate, and lost the key. No one mistreats your pup or mine.

One final point: The kennel operator must consent to administering any medicine Pup will require while you are gone. And he takes the phone number of your vet and agrees to call if anything goes—or looks—wrong. No ifs, ands, or buts.

Ask around. You'll find someone who knows what type of operation each boarding kennel maintains. And good luck.

OUT WALKING PUP

Pueblo, Colorado, paramedic Jim Partin was heeling his Grand Hunting Retriever Champion, golden retriever Dolly, beside his horse as he cantered across a broad expanse of cut wheat fields.

But suddenly he saw angling toward them, at very high speed, a semiwild dog. Jim ordered Dolly to sit, hoping the dog would give up all interest in a placid target—but no! The dog hit Dolly so hard, it tore her left rear leg as she was sitting. And to this day Dolly must drag that leg. What a noble gal she's been. What heroic deeds she attained to get her championship. And to be done in by a half-wild runaway thing that was turned loose by uncaring people and couldn't help becoming a renegade.

So what's the point to this story? Carry a cane or staff when you walk Pup, folks, to ward off any attackers. I don't know a community that doesn't have a leash law by now; no dog is supposed to be running loose. And though you may have to defend yourself in court, you can assuredly prove self-defense, because any fool could see that the dog was running loose in defiance of the leash law.

GOOD HOUSEKEEPING

Be a thoughtful neighbor. If you're walking in a residential neighborhood, pick up all Pup's potty and carry it home. To be truly carefree, try to get Pup into the country, where you don't have to worry about offending anyone.

Farmers are asked for access all the time by hunters. Think how novel they would regard your request that you merely be permitted to walk your dog.

GOING TO THE VET

When taking Pup to the vet walk him on a leash, or if he is small enough, carry him in your arms. After you tell the receptionist your business, what's wrong, and who you want to see, have her make a notation that you have brought and are leaving a leash so you can get it back. How many have I lost at a clinic?

A vet clinic is a place housing disease. I dread taking a dog there, dread him having to walk on that floor. But it's got to be done.

Make sure you keep Pup distant from any other entering canine patients. We don't want a dogfight.

Same goes for cats.

Keep moving Pup about if you're left in the entry room. We don't want somebody bending over and going, "Coo, coo, coo," and Pup snapping her finger. If a rambunctious child appears, get Pup up in your lap even if he's a Great Dane. We don't want an unattended child nipped. Another lawsuit.

If the receptionist puts you in an examining room and tells you that the doctor will be a few minutes—then leave the clinic. These places are horror chambers for Pup; he's already terrorized by being there. Get him into the fresh air, walk him down the block, go sit in your car. Never, never, never just let him sit in an examining room and imagine—in his little head—the worst. For that's what he's doing.

Some clerk will often stop you, saying, "Where are you going?" You tell her. Whereupon she tells you that's not their policy, that you'll have to stay where you were put, and on and on.

I tell such people, "When they voted on that policy, I wasn't here. So I just voted, and Pup and I are going for a walk."

When leaving your dog at the vet's office, any examining-room exchange, from you to the vet, must be done fast. Tell the doc what's wrong and leave. For you see, once you turn the dog over and disappear, all the shaking stops. You're no longer there for the dog to plead to for support, so now he begins working on whoever takes him. Dogs are smart, and very capable of ingratiating themselves with whomever you leave them with.

I realize vets can run overtime with emergencies. That's fine with me: My dog may be the next one needing fast and capable treatment. But that still doesn't mean Pup has to endure a long wait in an examining room. It's not fair to him, it's stressful, and there have to be alternatives.

14

What the World Needs Now Is Love, Sweet Love

I was five years old and had a bad reaction to a smallpox vaccination. It was during the Depression and there was scant heat in the house, less food, and no money. Mother stood at the end of the bed and wrung her hands. Then she hoped—she dared—by saying, "If you'll get well, Billy, I'll buy you a red kite." Immediately I bucked up, but kites cost a nickel. How could she afford it? But she went me one better and bought the kite and slid it under my bed, saying, "Remember, get well enough to go outdoors and you can fly it." So what happened? I'm writing this book. Ha!

I'm so busy getting Pup fed, housed, and trained that I've drifted from the purpose of this book: the Magic of Dogs.

We now know that pups sense feelings and dogs eventually learn language. And we are further aware that many dogs in the past obeyed out of fear, but our pup pleases us because he doesn't want to disappoint us. And why is this? Because he's a love-trained dog and he's bonded. And love-trained dogs regard our expression of hurt or disappointment more painfully than if we'd hit them with a club.

Now this technical stuff in the last chapters is necessary, but it's not why we have dogs in our lives. Besides, if we take our time, Pup will learn at his leisure, and on his own, all we've tried to formally teach.

And in order to run you through the training section quickly, I did not repeat our truth that pups sense meaning in us more than they understand us. Dogs—that's different. They eventually learn language and mix that knowledge with the perception they have of us. So you must remember this. Pup will learn what you want him to do by feedback, FIDO. To train or not to train? That's up to you. Me? I'd say the heck with it because I don't want Pup to ever feel that you're the heavy.

GIRL TALK

It's Memorial Day morning. Dee's up—as always. I awaken and ease my feet from the bed to feel around for my slippers. Arthritics suffer what's called morning stiffness. If I kneel down to look under the bed I'll become a beached whale. So I yell, "Mom, the girls have taken my slippers."

She arrives to kneel down, shaking her head. Then she hands me the slippers and says, "What would you do without me?" I reply, "I pray to God I never find out."

Dee stands, changing the subject by saying, "Muffy wouldn't get out of bed."

Dee's taking Muffy's near-death very hard, so I wish to change the subject as I ask, "Where's Candy?"

"She just jumped on the floor . . . she slept wrapped around your head."

I reach down for Candy to love her, but Puddin runs a wet nose under my wrist, lifting it, appropriating it for herself. Candy rockets from under the bed, growling. She's the hammer, and nobody steals her privileges. Puddin licks Candy's mouth to seek a truce and, like a kid would do, Candy roots her mouth along on the carpet as if to say, "Ick!"

Chili's bark comes from the back of the house. "She's out there surveying her Las Vegas nothingness," Dee tells me. "She thanks God we had the money to send her to camp this summer." Dee's referring to our short stay in Sedona, where the national forest abuts our property line and the federal wilderness area where the dogs and I wander starts three-quarters of a mile distant.

And that's the way our lives go. Dee and I gauge the world and discuss it through our girls. We've had many. So someone, or something, will always remind us of one of them. The dogs become a shorthand for us to discuss the world we live in.

The other day, Dee ran into a 7-Eleven for a diet Coke. When she got back to the car, she was all smiles as she gushed, "You should have seen that beautiful little girl in there. Blue eyes, long blonde hair. And she had on one pink slipper and one purple one." Dee mentioned that little girl again and again most of the day. But it was actually Candy she was talking about. For Candy would be that sassy, that confident, that capable if she'd been a human instead of a canine. Only Candy would have chewed up the slippers.

And so it goes. Any sultry, long-haired couch-gal is Sugar. For Sugar has that disinterest in the world . . . and she is beautiful. I call her Rhonda Fleming (remember that gorgeous red hair?) and once I asked Dee, "Why don't the guys call on Rhonda?"

And Dee answered, "Because they know you'd kill them."

Chili is like the old woman you see written up on plaques these days who wants a purple dress and a red hat when she gets old. That's how much a part of the world Chili lives in. We read about some gal walking across the Kalahari Desert. That would be Chili—anything to escape. That's why she's out there on the back patio now, dreaming of jungles.

Punk, the westie, had the determination of a bulldozer. She could spend a whole day stalking a mouse. Never moving. Never even twitching. She could have been a reincarnation of Sacajawea who led Lewis and Clark up the Missouri, only she would have hunted and filled their larder as well. When it comes to perseverance, we always remember Punky.

Pooder, the mongrel terrier buried in Sedona, made the one-thousand-mile trip from our Kansas farm to Phoenix. She sat in that old blue Oldsmobile station wagon on the fat armrest and gazed into the unknown. Pooder had everything required of an Amelia Earhart, staring from that cockpit for days at an endless expanse of ocean. And she had another dimension. She could have been a wonderful grandmother because she let Dee's nieces dress her in ragtime clothes and a pair of Kmart sunglasses. Poody did it.

So all our dogs give us insight and reference to life, plus verbal pictures with which to discuss it.

A DESERT DRIVE

When we traveled all day from our Las Vegas rental to our home in Sedona, Tiff upchucked; the rest did fine. It was hot, though, and we were all used up when we got here. It is a fact, folks: Coming down the road with six dogs and all their equipment in two cars does make us look like something right out of *The Grapes of Wrath.*

But who cares what people think? So long as Dee and I and the kids are happy.

Dee says, "They really enjoy this house. They've been running this morning. Around and around the sofa, then down the hall, and back again." I nod, for Dee's talking about more than she's saying. She hates Las Vegas. She and I built this place and never intended to leave. Sank all our savings into it. And we built it specifically for dogs with coyote-proof walls in back, snake-proof gates, puppy-proof fences in front, dog doors, a vet table in the laundry room, and on and on.

"And they like this cool weather," Dee continues, "but don't we all?"

"And how's the Muffy girl?" I ask.

I'm told, "She's fine . . . she lost that big belly you gave her last night with that saline flush. Now she looks slim as a puppy."

The puppy remark comes about because we've never seen Muffy like this before. Lynnette Tapia, the Las Vegas groomer, shaved Muffy, and now she looks so small.

Dee always admired Muffy's long, flowing hair, but it got matted. It all happened during this illness when we were more concerned with keeping her alive than keeping her groomed. So the matted hair came off like thick patches of wool. Lynn was nice about it though, as she let me hold up Muffy's back end so she'd not be weight-bearing. Ever since her herniated disk, we've never known how long Muffy's rear end would last.

Muffy's back was useless after surgery and we had to put a towel under her belly to hold her up and help her learn to walk again. And she couldn't hold her urine or her stool because of neural damage, so the vet taught me how to express her—to empty her bladder—and that way we could get through the night without her wetting in the bed.

Remember this! Vets meet so many people who are lackadaisical or just flat don't care about their animals—especially those who gripe about the cost of needed medical care—that if they find a conscientious, or even an interested, pet owner, they'll go the extra mile to help. Same with the groomer. Lynn let me into her domain, whether or not it hindered her work.

Dee continues, "It's so nice here." I'm silent, for there's nothing I can say. But I have resolved that we will gather up our duffel and throw it in our old diggings.

Dee observes, "Candy is doing her nails again." What she's talking about is Candy's allergies. She licks her paws. And when we see that, we talk in terms of cosmetics.

"Well, it's not the tick spray," I tell her. "I washed that good into the soil."

Since Dee is their protector and defender and apologizer, she'll find some reason for their paw licking—and I don't want it to be me.

Why do I take your time to relate the goings-on of our inconsequential household on a Memorial Day morning? To emphasize that we don't keep dogs, *we live dogs.*

On Your Becoming Dog

Dogs are the central focus of our lives. Our main interest, our primary conversation, our ultimate concern.

Except for God and our love for each other, they provide whatever enrichment, pleasure, sense of duty, happiness, and warmth we have.

And that's what I want to convey to you—I want you to have the same heightened interest and value in your life.

There's nothing on earth that brings the satisfaction of a large brood of dogs. Nothing. And the more you have, and the longer you have them, and the more you interact with them, the more contributory they become.

Don't you see? *You become dog!*

That is, dogs gradually mold your makeup. In a way, you become a product of the dogs. Think what that means. To be faithful, and just, and caring, and loving, and compassionate. In other words, you become kind like a dog, solicitous like a dog, caring like a dog.

The dentist was amused the other day when he entered the room late and found me asleep in his chair. I told him, "I learned it from the dogs . . . when there's nothing going on, go to sleep." I could also have told him I learned never to betray a friend, always to protect a loved one, and always to keep the faith.

Watching Faces

Modern man has a ton of faults. Modern dogs don't.

All the Tarrants love Christmas. Here Candy celebrates her first one by tearing up gift wrapping.

I go to the grocery and look at the faces of some people. Why are they so mad? What has made them look so mean? They glare at you. They are cocky, sullen, and act like they want to fight.

I wrote this chapter just to put us all back in perspective. We can train right, feed right, house right, treat right. That's great. But what's the point?

It's much more important to me that you have a friend. That you have a friendly open heart at your front door when you come home.

And the truth is this—hell, this book is this: Just live with your dog, love your dog, make him central to your life, and you will create the best friend you ever had . . . in an age when we need one most.

Remember: Dogs are therapeutic. They heal, they soothe, they release tension, they lower heartbeats and blood pressure and this twenty-first-century sense of doom most people have.

Doctors say, "Take two aspirins and call me in the morning." They should say, "Go to the pound, get two dogs, and you'll never have to call me again."

So we've had this time out and now let's get back to the nuts and bolts of caring for Pup. It was good taking a break with you. Just remember: I never had a dog in my life who didn't turn out to be a red kite. After reading this book—my hope is—neither will you. A pup will give you back your life.

PART THREE

BREEDING, WHELPING, NUTRITION, AND VETERINARY CARE

15

BREEDING

Whenever a dog becomes the national champion, everyone wants kingdom's seed. So an admirer sent a bitch to be bred. But the champ had fallen on bad times—he was being ignored by his trainer, becoming tick- and flea-infested, filthy, unnoticed, and depressed. The would-be breeder then learned from kennel help that the old champ could no longer mate. The champ's owner was informed, and he immediately rescued the dog from the kennel and took him to the vet. He told the vet the old dog would no longer breed, and the vet—looking at the dog—said to the owner, "If you were in that condition, would you?"

DR. ROYSE

Doc Royse has taught me dogs for thirty-five years. At first he ordered me a vet's case, then stocked it with stuff an outbackman would need a hundred miles from town. Then on weekends, or sometimes at night, he'd invite me to his clinic and show me how to use everything: splints, needles and thread, syringes, tourniquets, snake-bite serum. There was no charge.

As the years went by Doc would come to the farm and sit in the kitchen and we'd talk about ailments, the state of the vet art, the ethics of the profession, the overabundance of vet graduates, the intense competition that started during the 1970s. Or there would be times he'd call and I'd accompany him on out-clinic runs. One client had a hundred Brittanies at a game preserve, and we'd go every six months and give the dogs physicals and shots.

Dr. Royse was my James Herriot. Know who that is? Herriot is the pen name of an English vet who became lionized for his inspired writings on human understanding and animal care. His books even became the basis for the PBS TV series "All Creatures Great and Small." Herriot was the epitome of the rural, one-man practice, highly competent and caring. Later in this book we will ask—but fail to answer the question—is James Herriot dead? The average American will be surprised at why we can't answer the question.

Doc Royse is America's James Herriot: equally bright, compassionate, humane, and caring. And, like Herriot, Royse talks so you can understand him. The world is full of vets (and MDs) who talk in megasyllables that signify nothing to the average person. Which is to say, they can't (or they won't) communicate. Remember? *That which is shared equally by two or more.* When these medics talk, they share nothing. When Doc Royse talks, we share everything.

I've told Royse that our topic is breeding, so he crosses his legs, rears back in the office chair, and says, "The breeding of dogs is both an art and a science. And you'd be amazed—and you'd be amused—at the notions I've heard presented here in my clinic. Old wives' tales, mostly, but they're all fascinating. And, by golly, if some of them don't have a kernel of truth in them. But a man's judgment is only as good as the information on which it is based, so let's see if we can't come up with some stuff for all those people out there.

"Let's face it, a guy or gal usually wants a pup out of old Pard, or they want a pup out of that bitch because she's the best dog they ever had, or they want to raise a litter of pups for their friends. Those are the reasons for most dog matings. And we need to help these people get that pup.

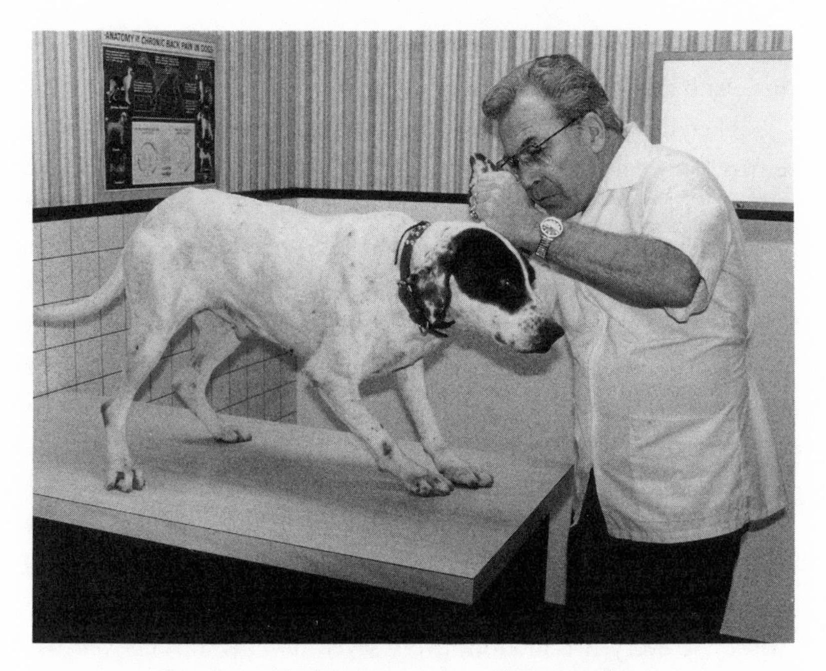

Doc Royse checks a tense pointer for ear problems.

THE FEMALE

"To start with, we'll talk about the female. Most of the time, people want to know when to breed their dog. A bitch will usually not cycle the first time until she is six to nine months of age, but it will vary from dog to dog. It's not a good idea to breed that first heat; the dogs are not skeletally mature—haven't got their full growth. I always think it's a good idea to wait for the second cycle.

"Heat is a four-stage process, consisting of (in scientific, or medical terms) proestrus, estrus, metestrus, and anestrus. But the average person doesn't recognize each of these cycles. Proestrus is the first sign of heat, characterized by swelling of the vulva and a watery red discharge. Sometimes bitches will start to attract males, but they won't let them mount.

"The estrus period for the heat cycle is marked by a more copious blood-tinged discharge, though sometimes it will turn a little straw color. The bitch will flag her tail to the side and will stand for the male and allow him to mount and breed.

"Then there is the metestrus cycle, which immediately follows the estrus for a period of two months. This is described as the period when the bitch has hopefully conceived and all the hormones are going back to the level for conception and carrying of puppies. This lasts a couple of months and this is the stage when you'll sometimes see false pregnancy. Because even if they don't mate, their hormonal makeup starts up the mammaries, which sometimes stimulates the maternal instinct to the point where she'll have a false pregnancy for you.

"Anestrus is that time between cycles (about three months). The normal bitch will cycle anywhere from six to nine months. We say twice a year—which is right—but unfortunately, you can't depend on a dog to do it regularly. In other words, you might have a dog who will cycle every five months, every seven months, or one who will cycle now and five months later and seven months after that. So it's a general thing.

"Now, to put all this medical jargon into the way I personally talk about things: The old rule of thumb on a heat cycle is eighteen to twenty-one days from start to finish. A week coming in, which would be proestrus, a week for estrus, and a week going out, which would be metestrus."

KEG OF BLACK POWDER

As Doc talks I glance out the farm window and in my mind's eye I see the brilliant, world-class bitch, the Labrador retriever Keg of Black Powder, dash across the lawn. Powder was Jim Culbertson's big-time field-trial champion. She's buried in back of the farm, east of the dam.

Jim had no money to campaign Powder, for in those days he made $4,000 a year coaching the Mulvane, Kansas, high-school football team. He once turned down an offer to sell her to a wealthy field-trial patron for $16,000, four times Jim's annual salary from coaching.

Catch as catch can, Jim and I kept Powder on the campaign trail. Then she qualified for the National. But fate stepped in: Powder came into heat.

Well, a female dog can't run in a field trial if she's in heat. It puts the males off their game. So Jim took Powder to a vet where she received a newly available shot to prevent her heat cycle. The result? Powder was never right again. She became squirrelly, disoriented—no longer the athlete who the experts anticipated would win the trial she now could not attend.

So I guess the lesson in all this is that heat is a mysterious and powerful thing, deeply driven, demanding to surface. And in those days, at least, something no man should mess with.

THE MATING

Doc Royse continued, "Most bitches will very seldom accept a male that first week. I usually tell people to put their male with the female on the ninth day after noticing the bitch coming into season. I say that because it's usually somewhere between that ninth day and the fourteenth day that the bitch will stand for breeding. And there again, this is where it seems to be more of an art than a science, for you'll get a female who won't stand until the sixteenth day.

"After you've got a mating in that ninth- to fourteenth-day period, don't abandon precautions until that dog is completely out of heat . . . which would be the eighteenth to twenty-first day. Because, by golly, you'll get a female now and then who'll stand for a male twelve straight days, and you don't know exactly what day—or days—they mated. So, you need to put a little common sense with it and know your dog after she set her cycles.

"So those are the basic time frames and the process of the female cycle: coming into season, mating, and going out of season."

The Importance of Time

"The problem I find most with people is that they don't mark down the dates when the female was bred. They'll say, 'Well, I think they bred . . . oh, gosh, around the fourth of July somewhere. . . .' Considering that the gestation period is only sixty-three days, if you're off five days, that's a tremendous disparity in time for a vet to make a decision if this bitch is in trouble: When is she supposed to whelp? So I tell people, 'I don't care how many times she mated, or if you think she mated that day—write it down.'

""Then the vet has got a key to work with when you bring this bitch in and say, 'I think she's due and she's not doing anything.' For a vet to try to guess if she's three days early or three days late . . . you're reading a crystal ball.

"It's usually about thirty-five days after the mating that you can tell if the dog's pregnant by examination, by palpation. Unfortunately, there is no biological test for pregnancy; they've been working on it for a long time, but it has just not come down the pike."

Concerns While Mating

"About the actual mating—it all depends on the male and female. No way can you just throw them together and leave them. If the female won't stand, she can attack the male. Besides, the male is in a constant state of hypertension and stress all this time.

"Bring them together and see what the female's response is. If it's no good, then separate them far enough so the male can't smell the female. Now bring them back together a day or two later. Keep testing. Finally, when the female does stand, get at least two good matings to ensure conception."

Runaway Judy

This time my mind captures a diabolic scene. I was overseeing Judy's mating in her kennel run. Judy was a huge Labrador retriever, slightly hyper, too fat, with a head the size of a pumpkin. But lacking looks, Judy had an uncanny ability to endure ice water. This was something I wanted to preserve in a breeding.

Anyone with a dog is going to make mistakes. Remember when you do make a mistake, you suddenly twirl around hoping no one saw what happened, so you'll never have to answer for it?

Well, when that brought-on stud tied with Judy she bolted for her doghouse. The house had a small door. And yes, folks, Judy entered that door faster than a pitched ball strikes a catcher's mitt, and that stud was slammed against the wall above the door. I need say no more. The male entered Judy's house backward.

So the thing I learned was this: Never mate a bitch unless you've got total control of her. Henceforth, Judy was leashed to the chain-link in her kennel run anytime a male came to visit. But as Doc tells us now, maybe there was something physically wrong with Judy that caused her to bolt.

THE OBSTINATE BITCH

What about a bitch who won't mate or conceive?" Doc asks. "There are few bitches who are inherently poor breeders, and that's all there is to it. You can check these dogs out physically in every aspect, you can try every technique you want to in the world; they are what we call poor breeders, or shy breeders. And I don't know what we're seeing here. Pure genetics? A combination of psychic-physical things? There are some factors that can inhibit a bitch from standing for a male. If a bitch will stand for a male, but goes bonkers—screams and runs away when he attempts to mate her—you need to get her checked. Sometimes you'll find a bitch with a small vaginal opening: a small aperture to the vulva into the vagina. Many times that can be corrected surgically.

"Once in a while, you'll find a bitch with some little fibrous bands up in the vaginal vault . . . kind of like you had a garden hose with a toothpick stuck in it. I mean it's stuck. These can be taken out with little or no problem.

"And these two examples are probably the main two physical reasons that a bitch would act like that. But should you get bitches who will breed well, stand well, accept the male, and you can't get pups, then you have to look at both the male and female.

"Brucellosis is one thing you must always check them for. It can produce sterility in both the male and female. Brucellosis is not real common, except in large-dog populations. For the average guy who's got an average dog, this is not a common thing. But it's something you don't want to overlook.

"In the female, it's real difficult if there is a medical reason she won't conceive. It's very, very difficult to determine. Low-grade uterine infections, in which there may be no apparent symptoms, may do it. This can usually be checked out with some laboratory work to give you an indication.

"Ovarian malfunctions can also do it. Either the ovaries do not produce enough ova or they do not produce a high enough estrogen level to make the system work.

"You sometimes find during routine spays a cyst on ovaries; these interfere with ovarian function, but cause no other problem whatsoever with the dog. These dogs come in here at three years old to be spayed, and during the operation I pull up an ovary and—bingo—I've got a cyst the size of my thumb on it. The dog's not having any problem, but it plays heck with the ovarian function. And that's a real toughie to detect."

THE MALE

"If you're not getting pups, you've got to look at the male. There again you check for out-and-out sterility. Check the male for brucellosis, just like you do the female. He also should be checked for normal testicular size and shape. See that there isn't anything wrong, such as atrophy of the testicle—or even tumors. Check his prostate; a chronically infected prostate can cause trouble. Determine also (it's not common at all) if the male's organ cannot emerge through his prepuce. Check the preputial opening. Some of these dogs will develop a stricture in there.

"Then, if you're having trouble getting these dogs to mate, give them both a thorough physical examination. The status of their health is important. Obviously, if the dog is losing weight or not looking good, there might be a problem somewhere else.

"In the male, you also need a sperm count and evaluation. This can be done very simply by your veterinarian. He will tell you the numbers of the sperm, which is significant, the volume of the semen, also significant, and the shape and motility (movement) of the sperm, again significant. To summarize we need to check the testicles, prostate, prepuce, and sperm count on the male if we're having trouble.

As We Learned with Keg of Black Powder

"I sometimes have clients ask if there's anything we can do to stimulate mating. I'm not very satisfied or happy with anything that would enhance the breeding ability of a dog. Hormones don't do it, I don't think; if it's not in the dog to do it, there's nothing you can give him to make him do it. However, researchers are doing a lot of work on this. Colorado State University probably does more work than anybody on fertility in dogs. They're using hormones at certain intervals before the dog is to cycle either to enhance conception or to increase litter size. But so far there aren't any answers we can depend on."

As Doc pats his pockets to find his tobacco, I'll take this opportunity to warn you: Always be hesitant about giving your dog anything that is new on the market. Or anything that is advertised as overriding basic physiological functions.

The mating drive, and both the meeting and development of the female's egg and the male's sperm, seem impervious to man's tampering. Don't ever forget Powder.

And don't ever forget the little miniature poodle who was delivered to a veterinarian. The owner, a woman, was totally befuddled at how Crystal could have become impregnated. The vet asked if there were any males in the house. And the woman answered, "Oh yes, her twin brother. But he would never do a thing like that."

That's not the end of the story. The vet attempted to perform an abortion on Crystal. But alas, when her time came, she gave birth to two dead pups. This and other case histories tell me when it comes to my dogs at least, it's best not to mess with Mother Nature. If there's a pregnancy, go ahead and have the pups. There's always a child somewhere close by who needs a dog in his or her life.

Doc's pipe is stoked as he says, "There is one thing we should mention. In humans, we know there is a chemical repelling factor between sperm and ovum. We have every reason to believe that this can happen with dogs, but we have never studied this enough to know one way or the other. If you've got a proven bitch and a proven male—they've both produced pups with other mates—who can't conceive together, then I have to think this so-called chemical factor is at work."

THE HEAT CYCLE

"Now let's talk about stopping a heat cycle. I remember when one drug company came out with an antiheat shot. Within three to four years, veterinarians began to see uterine infections in bitches to whom this drug had been administered. So the drug was pulled from the market. It was followed by another drug that worked so long as you continued to give it, but the dog automatically came into estrus once you stopped giving the dog this drug.

"They're still working on it. And what most of them are concentrating on is putting something in the dog's food.

"But we've got two different concerns. One is aborting a pregnancy, and the other is keeping a dog from coming into heat.

"Now, there is an assumption among some veterinarians that you should be very cautious with using hormone drugs to abort a pregnancy in its early stages. Why? Because of your desire to breed this bitch later and not prompt any complications."

HORMONES

"There are two concerns that prompt this caution. First, when you put hormones into an animal, you have upset the hormone balance. Once you put a hormone in there, you have no control over it, and you don't know exactly how you're going to upset the hormone balance. That can create problems with future breedings.

"Second, there is some degree of risk. It is not really terribly prevalent, but it is a consideration because some of these hormones can cause blood dyscrasia [any of various intestinal inflammations] or anemia. But I admit I don't see a lot of it.

"The bottom line today, with the present state of the art, is if you mess with nature's cycle you can be looking at future problems.

"Now let's consider stacking. Hormones have a cumulative effect with chronic repeated doses.

"Take cortisone or prednisone. Every animal's metabolism is different, but the result is the suppression to some degree of the adrenal glands. The worst scenario is where the adrenals won't function. The adrenal glands produce cortisol, hydrocortisol, adrenaline, and aldosterone, so now we're talking about real problems. Cortisones also suppress the immune system.

"Now to something else. Many breeders ask about a biological test for verifying a pregnancy. We've sure got it for horses, cattle, and humans, but unfortunately many of these tests depend on levels of certain hormones, and a false pregnancy in the bitch may nullify them. Immunological tests have just not proven out yet. There just isn't such a thing."

ARTIFICIAL INSEMINATION

"As for artificial insemination: It can be done and there's a reasonable degree of success to it. It all depends on the skill of the technician and on the dog. You've got to handle the semen very carefully. Extreme sterile conditions, rapid transport from the male to the female, and the volume of the semen you can get from a male are all factors.

"Unfortunately, the anatomy of the bitch is such that it does not lend itself to getting that semen as high up in the vagina as we'd like. Horses and cattle are pieces of cake, but the dog has a funny little anatomy in that vagina that doesn't allow you to do that as well. I don't have statistics on success, but I've not had better than 50 percent here in my clinic.

"Here's an odd fact that many of your readers may not know about. If you've got a group of bitches you are breeding in a kennel, it is not uncommon for those bitches to cycle together. Bitches housed together eventually cycle at approximately the same time. Also, when new bitches are introduced to the kennel, their heat periods will eventually coincide approximately with the other bitches. We don't know why this is. Apparently, it must have something to do with some type of psychic stimulation."

THE TIE

"Now let's consider the tie. A male and female will tie from seven to eight minutes up to fifteen minutes or more. This is nature's way of enhancing conception; all during the tie the male continues to produce and deposit semen in a more-or-less closed cavity. The sperm are very motile and very, very active, and since the tie prevents the male from backing out, the sperm immediately begin to gravitate up and into the uterine tract toward the fallopian tubes where hopefully they will meet an ovum.

"So the tie accomplishes two things. First, you can be positive that the dog has deposited his sperm as high up in the vagina as he can; second, you can be sure you've got a good mating. Dogs certainly can impregnate a bitch without tying, but the nice thing about the tie is you know you've got a good mating.

"In breeding, the worst thing you can do is to take both dogs into unfamiliar territory. I have people call me and ask if they can mate their dogs at my clinic. I always say no because when a dog comes into this place and gets one smell of this medicine, instinctively he's *suppressed*."

Remember my taking my dog from the examining room? I told the clerk I'd walk the streets until the vet could see me. Doc has just told you why I do it. His word is *suppressed*.

"I tell these people to mate," says Doc, "at either the bitch's premises or the male's premises. One or the other. Then at least one of the dogs is on familiar ground."

Remember Delmar Smith with the ten national Brittany champs? Delmar would teach his male champions to breed on command. And their incentive was buttressed by Delmar always putting the mating pair in a horse trailer. Delmar was always trialing on horseback, so the trialer would always be handy. It worked.

IN CONCLUSION

Doc grows silent. He thinks. He looks about his office.

Doc finally says, "Well, Bill, that's about it. But there is one last thought. The breeder who's ahead is the one who's had his dogs long enough to know their cycles. Now he can plan things. He knows that if he has several breeding bitches, they likely will all come into season the same time.

"This is a mess because the males must all be brought in at the same time, and the puppies are born at the same time, and all must be disposed of in short order. But it's no chore for the observant breeder who understands these things and plans in advance."

THE ENHANCEMENT OF THE BREED

Doc is a scientist. He knows medicine and he clinically knows the dog. But there's another aspect of breeding and it has nothing to do with egg or sperm or tie or anything like that.

How do you breed to develop the spectacular dog? That's the question every serious dog man and dog woman continually asks.

I'll give you an example: Bob Wehle of Midway, Alabama, the Field Trial Hall of Famer who's bred English pointers for sixty years, is the dean of dog experts in the twentieth century.

Bob's the quintessential man—geneticist, philosopher, dog trainer, sculptor, writer, and culinary genius. But he mumbles things, and when you try to pin him down he gets evasive. That's because of his innate modesty.

Because of this, Bob reminds me of when I was eight years old and I caught an eel in the creek south of the waterwheel-driven flour mill at Oxford, Kansas. That slippery, elastic, contorting thing defeated me. That's Bob.

Well, Bob and a friend were walking through his kennels in 1990. And Bob pointed toward a pup and told the visitor, "This is going to be the best dog I ever bred. I call him Snakefoot—got it from the movie *Dances With Wolves.* He will win the National Shooting Dog Championship."

Bob later told Tom Davis, the gifted dog writer for *Pointing Dog Journal,* that Snakefoot was the finest dog he ever bred and he would win a major championship. Tom wrote it up in the September/October issue, 1993.

Then wham! Just like that, in early 1995, Snakefoot won the National Shooting Dog Championship *and* the Masters Championship, back to back.

When I reminded Bob about his prediction he tried to deflect my inquiry. He would only say, "I was very brash, you know. To predict a win like that would be the same as predicting a foal would win an eighty-four-horse Kentucky Derby."

Precisely! And he did it.

It took Bob Wehle sixty years to point to a pup in a kennel and tell an onlooker that this dog was going to sweep the field. And folks, that's the bottom line in breeding: the enhancement of the breed—to develop a better dog to aid the blind, drive the sheep, sniff out the bomb, find the bird, or do any of the myriad things our contemporary dog is asked to do. And, not just to do it, but to predict it.

Breeding is a science, but it is also an art, or an intuition, if you will. Suffice to say there's hardly a breeder in a million who can call his shot like Wehle. You'll find books on breeding in the library to inform you about this aspect of dogs.

Doc Royse is standing now and I walk out the farmhouse with him. I thank Doc for giving us his afternoon off; he could have gone hunting or fishing. That would have fulfilled him, but instead, he fulfilled us.

16

Puppy Survival

It was 1955, and a Dr. E. R. Calame of Jonesboro, Arkansas, had a white-and-liver pointer on the field-trial circuit handled by professional trainer Leon Covington of Calhoun, Alabama. Cov (as he was called) was also an excellent amateur golfer. The story goes, Cov was campaigning Calame's dog in Union Springs, Alabama, and wanted to compete in a golf tournament in Georgia. But his scout, an old black man, told him, "Mr. Cov, if I had a dog as good as you got, I'd run him in Grand Junction if I had to walk him there." Cov passed up the golf tournament and headed for Tennessee. His dog, Lone Survivor—the only pup out of seven to survive a kennel fire—won the national. That's the name of the game, you know. Surviving!

You'd buy a used car from Jake Mosier, what with his Andy Griffith "shucks, fellows" smile, the soft voice, the shy manner.

I can see and hear him now: "Folks, this '64 Ford was owned by a demolition-derby driver who drank heavy and used the rig to hunt coyotes in outcrop rock country."

Next morning fifty people would appear to bid on the Ford. It had to be a sleeper: After all, the Silver Fox never misled or misdealed anyone. Silver Fox? Sure. Like a fox he can think running. Like Andy Griffith, there's that chrome gray hair.

But Jake Mosier doesn't sell used cars, nor win court cases on TV. Jake's into dogs. He may be the top dog man of his type in the world. He's Dr. Jacob Mosier, head of the veterinary school at Kansas State University. And Doc's decidedly specific: His specialty in veterinary medicine is keeping puppies alive from inception through weaning.

We're walking around his lab facilities at Kansas State as Dr. Mosier tells us, "People say to me, 'Why not let a pup that a mother shoves out of the nest die? That's just Mother Nature's culling. Why not get rid of the weak? That's the best thing that could happen to the breed.' "

Then this hands-on scientist answers himself, saying, "I'm convinced that the majority of the reason why that puppy is not doing well is not due to some inherited factor. That pup's sick because of his size, his nutrition . . . things we can possibly do something about.

"I came into this world weighing a little over four pounds—in the middle of a western Kansas blizzard—delivered by my dad, who was listening to my grandmother on the phone as to what to do next. I survived. So I feel the same way about runt pups. They'll survive, too, if we know what to do and care enough to do it."

We reach Doc's office where he sits at his desk and tells us, "Not all I tell you stems from my own research. What I've accumulated is information from a lot of people who've done a lot of work. Some of it in England, Belgium, this country. . . . "

How Good Are the Parents?

"On the basis of this and the work done at Bar Harbor, Maine, we can now state the obvious: The first determination to make so far as raising healthy puppies is selection of the sire and dam.

"Too often this selection is made on conformation or performance. Such qualities are important, but temperament is of equal if not greater importance.

"Also, reproductive capability has a heritable quality. Does the stud produce true, is the bitch a good brood matron? People don't consider these things. Also, are the parents disease-resistant? There's so many things we know we must watch for these days.

"Now assuming we've kept track of all this and picked a sire and dam as good as we can then the strength and vigor of the resulting pups will depend on the *mother's nutrition.* Animal protein is imperative in a puppy's diet. Now, there have been a number of research projects on this.

"A man developed as nearly perfect a feed as he could. Feeding this, his loss in puppies before weaning ranged from 40 to 80 percent. And if you think this is high, then I'll say to you you're not keeping accurate records of your own litter losses. Litter losses do run this high.

"Anyway, this man took the same diet and did nothing more than add some liver, and he was able to save about 80 percent of all his pups. Indicating, of course, the time-honored knowledge that liver is a good supplement. Those who wish to use liver should give an ounce per meal to the dam three times a week."

LIVER/BRAIN RATIOS

"Now another man working with sheep took ewes and divided them into two groups, bred them, and put one group on an excellent diet. He put the other group on a marginal diet. He wanted to see what effect ewe nutrition would have on resultant lambs. Lambs from the poorly fed ewes were half the size at birth as lambs from the enriched-fed ewes.

"Then this man looked at the lambs' organs and found that those organs most affected were the liver, the spleen, and the thymus [a gland that secretes some very complex hormones that regulate growth]."

"Well, in the early 1950s, we made the observation that liver/brain ratios have a great deal to do with the vigor and health of puppies. But people ignored this. Then in the mid-1960s an article out of Bar Harbor said: 'Runt pups have abnormal liver/brain ratios.'

"We picked this up and over the next ten years probably checked a thousand puppies' liver/brain ratios and I'm now convinced if we have a small puppy, a runted puppy, one who doesn't develop in the first three weeks, we can almost wager that he's going to have an abnormal liver/brain ratio.

"We learned the liver mass must be one and a half times larger than the size of the brain. Anything less than this, and I'll say to you, 'That puppy will never survive.' And I will further say, 'The reason why this occurs is not the sire or the dam, but purely the nutrition provided to the pup during his mother's pregnancy.'

"But you'll say back, 'Yet some of the litter are normal-size and they do well. How come?' "

THE PLACENTA

"Well, eight to ten years ago an article in the newspaper was headed BABY ELEPHANT BORN, and it went on to point out the baby weighed 260 pounds and the placenta weighted 60. Until that time, I'd never weighed the placenta of pups and related it to puppy size.

"Well, today I can tell you they're closely related. And this in turn relates directly to the nutrition the mommy supplied the pup while she was carrying him. And maybe where the pup was in line at birth.

"Now we still haven't checked this line thing out . . . but we do know the first puppy born is a fairly good size. He's not the runt. It's all probably related to the stacking in the uterus.

"And why is one placenta smaller than the other? We don't yet know. All we know is that a small placenta creates a small pup and that's directly related to the mommy's nutrition.

"Well, as we worked with these runt pups down through the years we tried to save them. Many would die in the first thirty-six hours. And within two weeks, 75 percent of all runt puppies would die. Now, why would they die?

"Quite a few reasons. The smaller ones, the weak ones, the ones who didn't have strong vigor, who weren't properly nourished during pregnancy, were *ineffectual nursers.* They'd get up there to the nipple and work a little bit, but they wouldn't really get anything down. They didn't quit nursing because they were full, they quit because they got tired.

"And if you open them up, you'll find that even though their stomachs look distended, they're filled with nothing but saliva and saliva bubbles."

THE INEFFECTUAL NURSER

"And why the ineffectual nurser? Such a pup has no strength of suction. Put your finger in his mouth, and he will just tongue it passively. There'll be no pull, nothing. Such a pup always feels like a limp dishrag in your hand; whereas a healthy pup feels like that old cigarette commercial: so round, so firm, so fully packed.

"As we looked at pups, we found they could be separated into three distinct groups during the first forty-eight hours: One group would start to gain weight at the twelfth hour. That's the majority of pups. But weighing them at twenty-four hours there'll be a subgroup that's lost less than 10 percent of their body weight. And there'll be another group that's lost more than 10 percent.

"Okay, those that have lost less than 10 percent will in all probability go on to gain weight. They'll survive. It's those that have lost more than 10 percent that are among the average 30 percent of a litter that dies.

"And the reason why this 30 percent doesn't gain weight is that the pups haven't taken any food in them. They're ineffectual nursers. And we've asked the question, 'Why is this?' And we have answered, 'There's muscle tone that must be considered, plus vigor, strength, size of pup, and the nutrition Mommy gave the pup during pregnancy.' "

The First Gasp

"But probably more important than all this is when this little puppy is first born . . . *his first gasp is life-and-death critical.*

"Now let's look at this first gasp. You deliver a baby, and I've seen this on television, they lift the babies up by the hind legs and swat them across the rump and the babies gasp and cry.

"Okay. What do these little puppies do? Well, when they're first delivered, the runts don't breathe very well. So we rub them, you know, and we pump them a little bit, and we turn them over and we swing them to empty the mucus out of their throats, and pretty soon they'll gasp a little bit.

"So we piddle with them a little longer, and pretty soon, maybe, they're breathing. You know, six, eight, ten times per minute. Well, that ol' puppy who doesn't take that first gasp—and/or it isn't a good one—never does distend the lungs to their full capacity. And this is important. *That puppy never gets another gasp chance.* He only gets one gasp in life, and his life depends on it.

"Now, if that puppy doesn't get a good first gasp, then from that point on he's hypoxic. He can't get enough oxygen to supply the muscles of his body and will never have the muscle tone he requires. Which, in turn, means he'll be an ineffectual nurser.

"So, somehow, we've got to get that first gasp to be a good one. It's even been worked out, you know, that it takes a burst of air that would raise water in a tube twenty-three centimeters [nine inches] to distend that puppy's lungs to full potential. And the capacity of those lungs is determined by the first gasp. But if the puppy has poor body vigor due to poor nutrition from his mommy and then he can't get oxygen to his bloodstream because he never had that first good gasp . . . then he just goes from bad to worse.

"So that's one thing I'm sure creates the ineffectual nurser. That lack of oxygen because the pup never expands his lungs."

THE SEPARATED PLACENTA

"Now, the second thing with this little puppy that may prevent him from having enough oxygen is if he's delivered hind feet first or if the bitch starts to have a little greenish discharge just before she starts to have the pups. Whenever that green color appears, we know that the placenta has started to separate.

"Whenever the placenta starts to separate, we've reduced the amount of surface with which that bitch is exchanging oxygen with that puppy.

"When this is reduced to a certain point—and we don't know just what that tension is, but probably a drop of 10 or 12 percent of that placenta separates—at that point, that puppy's going to gasp. And if he's inside the birth canal, then he's going to inhale—or aspirate—some of the fluid."

If a pup's born feet first, that means he's in the birth canal for an undue amount of time. Consequently, it's in this contaminated environment—lots of fluids—where he may take his first gasp.

"If a pup's got a lot of mucus in his throat, he's going to inhale some of that. This cuts down on his respiratory capacity. And that pup will just never get enough oxygen to create good muscle tone.

"Well, one time I read about a woman who raised Pomeranians whelped under oxygen. She claimed this saved her one pup per litter."

OXYGEN

"That was the first time it dawned on me this was an important kind of thing. And our observations since that time have borne this out. Today we know that if you want to save pups, they must breathe well upon delivery.

"And how do we get this? I'm not sure. One of the old-time remedies to get that puppy to gasp is to stretch his rectum just a little bit. Of course if we overstretch it I think we can cause some real trauma that way, too. It's going to take just the right stretch.

"I think we should be able to devise some type of small balloon that would create a certain amount of pressure, and we could put that over the pup's muzzle and blow to distend those lungs.

"That would be after we got the foreign matter removed from his respiratory tract. All pups have a lot of fluid in their throats and they gurgle and you can hear that, you know. We've got to get that fluid out.

"One way is to stick a piece of plastic tubing back there with a rubber ball on it and aspirate. The other way is to swing the pup between our legs. You know, open his mouth and swing him so he can get that stuff thrown out. That's the way we usually give artificial respiration to a puppy, anyway. Just keep his tail pointing toward your body and swing him up and down.

"Of course, in the clinic, we can tilt the pup on a board in an incubator and give him oxygen. It's amazing how much fluid comes out of those lungs, and how much better the pup'll start to breathe once he starts getting good oxygen exchange—the tone comes back to his muscles, and he'll become an effectual nurser."

So Dr. Jake has told us the pup's life cycle may be modified by:

1. giving the dam a liver supplement during pregnancy to provide animal protein for the pups, and

2. helping pups get a good first gasp in life, thus distending their lungs to the maximum and guaranteeing good oxygen exchange, which further enhances muscle tone.

THE PREMATURE PUP

Now Doc tells us, "All dogs are born premature—eyes sealed shut, ears sealed shut. Why, they can't even walk until they're seventeen days or so of age. Nor can they urinate or have a bowel movement on their own for about the first sixteen days. The mother has to trig-

Dr. Mosier examines a newborn pup.

ger the processes by licking them, then gathers the waste on her tongue—which she swallows and carries to the outside of the nest through her own elimination.

"It's amazing, really. What a mess that nest would be if pups could relieve themselves at will from the moment of birth.

"Then, almost simultaneously with the puppy walking, he can start relieving himself on his own. And that's the time pups can move out of the nest."

GLYCOGEN

"But I digress. . . . What I want to point out is when this pup's first born he has very little glycogen [a form of sugar] storage in his muscles—compared to the foal, the calf, the pig. And the pig is especially a multilitter type. You know pigs get up and start to walk right away.

"But this little ol' puppy lies there and he can't even stand up, can't see, and can't hear very well. Well, that puppy doesn't have very much glycogen in his muscles. All his energy storehouse happens to be in his heart and liver. And this is one reason why liver size (ideally at least one and a half times the size of the puppy's brain) becomes very important to us. Because whatever energy he's got in reserve is right there.

"And if you take this little ol' puppy at three days of age and separate him from his mother and don't feed him . . . twenty-three hours after his last feeding, he develops low blood sugar, which can lead to shock.

"What I'm saying is in twenty-three hours, he's used up all his energy storehouse."

BODY HEAT

"When that pup's born, he's so premature, he can't even control his own body heat. All his heat comes from his mother. Another miracle: She can keep him alive in a snowbank. Now, if you take a pup from his mother, you've got to put him in an environment temperature of about 87 degrees in order to prevent his body temperature from dropping below 94 degrees—that's recorded with a rectal thermometer."

Incidentally, Pup's body temperature the first two weeks is 94–97 degrees, second to fourth week 97–99 degrees, and four weeks on, 100–101 degrees.

"Which means, then, that a pup can generate only seven degrees of heat above his environmental temperature. Which is also to say that an isolated pup in an environment below 87 degrees is in serious trouble.

"Take this puppy and put him in 75 degrees, and his temperature is going to drop below 94. And when it does, all kinds of bad things happen. . . . "

THE CHILLED PUPPY

"This becomes a chilled puppy. Remember how we used to wonder why a mother would push a pup out of the nest, out of the litter? Well, now we know. She shoves him to the side because of his low body temperature. She recognizes instinctively that something's wrong and wants him out of there. Why? We can only conjecture.

"But this is what's important: Anytime that a puppy's temperature drops below 94 degrees, he develops a paralysis of the digestive tract. To prove this point, working with pups whose body temperature is 78, we've given them warm formula—but ended up killing them.

"That's right. We thought we were being kind, but the pups died. Why? Due to paralysis of the digestive tract, that food doesn't go any place—it stays right in the stomach.

"Take one of these puppies and keep him in the same environment—and his body temperature's 78 degrees—and feed him warm formula, wait three hours, feed him again, wait three hours, feed him again, wait three hours, feed him again. When he dies, and die he will, open him up. All three feedings will still be in the stomach."

"Or feed him once, and twenty-three hours later, when the pup dies, open him up, and there'll be hemorrhage all around the stomach and big old clabbered milk that hasn't moved into the intestine, so the pup hasn't received any value from the feeding.

"And another thing we'll find with the chilled puppy is that his whole esophagus, instead of being a nice, tight little tube, is a big old sack. It's just completely relaxed. There's no way this pup could nurse. No suction. So the chilled puppy can't nurse, and even if he could, his paralyzed digestive tract could not process the milk. The chilled puppy literally starves to death.

"So the critical thing is to warm the pup up *before* we put him back on the bitch."

WARMING UP A PUPPY

"Now, warming up a pup is an interesting sort of thing. We can suspend him in water the same temperature as his body, then gradually add warm water. But that's a laborious, time-consuming chore. So we've placed pups on heating pads, under infrared lights . . . and almost invariably caused them to die. Why? Trying to warm them too fast.

"The first tissue we warm up is the outer skin, then the subcutaneous tissue, and the minute these cells start to warm up they need more oxygen.

"But what's happening? That little ol' puppy who's cold—78 degrees—his respiratory rate has dropped from about 30 down to about 4. His normal heart rate would be about 220, and it's now dropped down to about 60. And he's still cold in the center, and that's the delivery place for supplying oxygen.

"So if you warm him up on the outside, those cells need more oxygen and don't have it, and they die and cause hemorrhaging. This, in turn, kills the pup because we tried to warm him too fast. Because we didn't have the heart rate and respiratory rate we needed."

JIGGLE WHILE YOU WALK

"But if we warm the pup slowly . . . I was amused a few years back by a lady in the audience of a kennel club I was addressing. She told the group, 'I have a sheep-lined vest, and it has an inside pocket. And I put the puppy in there and go about my kennel cleaning.' She reasoned, 'First off, my body heat warms that pup up slowly, and secondly, it's just as important that I jiggle while I walk.'

"Well, she finally confessed that she stuck the puppy inside her brassiere. She was a big, buxom lady, and of course that's good radiant heat, and I suppose she did jiggle when she walked.

"So her point was well made. We can take one of these little ol' puppies and put him in an incubator and turn the rheostat down low and gradually bring the temperature back up. But if we let the pup just lie there, he develops a lot of congestion on the lower side. So we need to turn him over, rub him vigorously, every ten minutes or so, if we really want to save that pup.

"So the best way to warm a pup is to put him in an inside pocket and go about your work.

"When that pup's temperature rises to 94 or above—and now he's starting to breathe a normal rate, and has a normal heart rate, and now he also has the ability to get suction—and you put him in the whelping bin, the bitch will claim him, and he'll get dinner.

"In this regard, you'll note that a dam tries to save a pup before she culls him. She licks him to raise his body temperature with her warm tongue, plus the friction of the tongue jiggles and turns the pup's body about."

Thinking for but a moment, Doc then jumps track and says, "Do you know how to monitor a puppy? To determine how well he's doing?"

ACTIVATED SLEEP

Not waiting for an answer, he reveals, "One of the ways is by so-called activated sleep. You've seen these little ol' puppies sleeping and jerking . . . jerk all the time.

"Well, that's something else Mother Nature designed into the puppy. Because he's born so premature, his muscles are very poorly developed. You know, he can't even stand up. Consequently, he spends 90 percent of his time sleeping. So in order to get that puppy strong enough to eventually stand up and start walking—by the time he's seventeen days of age or so—Mother Nature devised *activated sleep.* And without that, that puppy would not be able to walk.

"People say, 'The puppy's dreaming.'

"Not so. But he *is* communicating. Communicating to you. Telling you he's doing pretty well.

"You can take a puppy and put him in the incubator and he might be thin and look kind of rough, you know, because you're not getting enough water into him, not enough food, or you might be giving him too much, and he's got diarrhea.

"But, nevertheless, so long as that pup's jerking while he's sleeping you can feel very comfortable about his future. He's not going to die. But let that activated sleep stop, and within twenty-four hours that's going to be a real sick pup. So, as far as I'm concerned, activated sleep is just a real good thing to go by."

WEIGHT GAIN

"Another monitor is weight gain. If we weigh a pup at birth and then weigh him daily, we like to see him gain weight every day. And a good, vigorous puppy will. He'll double his birth weight by the time he's nine days old. So that's the goal we shoot for.

"There's another way—and maybe too scientific—and that's to say that a puppy should gain 1 to 1½ grams per each pound of his anticipated adult weight each day. If he's going to weigh ten pounds when he's full grown, the puppy ought to gain twelve grams a day. If he's going to be an 80-pound dog, that puppy better gain 100 grams (3.527 ounces) per day during his first three or four weeks of life—to be growing at the right rate.

"And if that puppy doesn't grow—and you know since you're weighing him every day—you've got a sure sign things are not going well. That pup's not getting enough food, or he's not digesting his food, or something's abnormal. So if someone asks me for a monitor I tell them, 'weight gain.' "

LOW BLOOD SUGAR

"Now let's back up. We talked about weight gain and we talked about the chilled puppy. Okay. If you've got a cold puppy and you warm him up with your body heat—and jiggle him all at the same time—you can help that pup out even more by feeding him glucose.

"Pups are born with a little glucose, but when that's used up, they develop low blood sugar. As we've noted before, this takes about twenty-three hours after last nourishment.

"Now, the colder a pup is, the longer he can survive, because his metabolism is low and he isn't burning energy very quickly. But if we warm him up, we need to give him some energy producer. Thus, glucose.

"Glucose can be used in the pup's body without any metabolism whatsoever—all the pup has to do is absorb it. But table sugar? That's sucrose and has to be broken down. Thus, with sugar, some type of body activity has to occur before the intake can do any good.

"My preference in overcoming low blood sugar is, first, glucose, then honey, and next to that Karo syrup, and finally table sugar. But it usually isn't that critical. Any one of them is useful to get that pup's blood sugar up so he can have the energy he needs to fight for his life."

Dr. Jake's mind leaps to other facts and figures. He tells us that a bottle-fed pup usually gets diarrhea because he's overfed. That's right, the nipple's hole is too large. A pup's body weight is 82 percent water, whereas a dog's is only 69 percent. Pups therefore have a tremendous need for water on a per-pound basis, compared to the adult dog. Under normal conditions, an adult dog takes about 23 cubic centimeters [3/4 ounce] of water per pound per day. This pup's got to have 75 cubic centimeters [2 1/2 ounces]. He's got to have three times as much water per pound per day.

"And do you know what causes a swimmer? That's the flat-puppy syndrome, the spraddle-legged pup? Would you believe rigid suture lines in the skull?"

Doc Jake goes on and on. The sun is setting, and I've got miles to go to reach my kennel. I ease away, thanking him softly, knowing I've had the pleasure of meeting a man who's devoted his life to . . . puppy love.

Remember all he's said here. The pup you save because of Doc's knowledge may be that one in a million.

17

NUTRITION

In the old days, my working dogs ate nameless bulk food I picked up in bulk at a feed mill for $2.50 a hundred. Those days are gone forever. Today's dog has a variety of food offerings—from many excellent pet-food companies—as critically formulated as the menus provided astronauts. We can now buy foods specifically for pups, working dogs, sedentary dogs, sick dogs, and geriatric dogs. Here we present many food options and explain why they are available.

This could be the most important chapter in this book. For whatever you feed your dog can save him or kill him. It's that simple.

As a kid, I'd stand in Kennedy's corner grocery and covet the five-cent cans of Strongheart dog food. I remember the label depicting a smiling police dog. I wanted my coax-home strays to have the best, but never once did they get a can of Strongheart.

Making my way in the world of dogs I've stood in the kennel house at the A. G. C. Sage plantation near Alberta, Alabama, and pondered the great oven where they used to bake corn pone for the bird dogs.

I remember Field Trial Hall of Famer Ed Mac Farrior of Union

Springs, Alabama, telling me that during the 1920s, when he and his dad were working gun dogs in the summer on the Canadian prairies, they'd order shredded wheat by the boxcar-load from Niagara Falls. These shreds mixed with beef, Ed Mac still contends, are the best dog food ever fed.

Earlier than that the millionaire sportsman Paul Rainey of Cotton Plant, Mississippi, was killing a steer a day for his hundred-plus pointers, retrievers, and bear dogs. Remnants of the outdoor oven stand today.

And I recall learning that Er Shelley of Columbus, Mississippi, was the first man to ever prepare commercial dog food. His formula was based on the fact that his dogs were getting the staggers on traditional food—but he never did. So he fed them what he ate.

And that's the way it went. Catch as catch can.

But no more.

Now, I can assure you, the commercial food scientifically prepared for dogs today gives them a more nutritionally balanced diet than you and I eat. It's now a fact: Our dogs are better fed than we are. And this is why:

DIETARY MANAGEMENT

This is a miraculous new era in veterinary medicine. It is now possible to prevent many terminal dog diseases, achieve cures for others that heretofore required surgery, and happily sustain the lives of some dogs who are living at death's door due to failing vital organs—*all through diet.*

This is all part of the new science of veterinary nutrition, which is the practice of dietary management (DM). DM is the control of the daily nutrient intake of both the healthy and the sick dog in order to increase the degree of health to prevent illness and to extend life. DM involves two fields. One, to practice preventive health care by carefully recognizing the scientific needs of the dog through his various stages of life and changing his diet accordingly. Plus, there is the science of enhancing a sick dog's response to therapy by changing his diet.

There is an expert who is employed by a specific dog-food company. The reason I will quote him is he's the only such expert to ever knock on my door and say he wanted to visit. And he didn't come once, he came twice, and I met him repeatedly at various veterinary conventions and conferences around the nation. If any other dog-food company had sent a representative—or if anyone had talked to me at those meetings—that expert would also be included in this chapter.

So this man works for Hill's Pet Nutrition, Inc., of Topeka, Kansas, but that is not important to me, the man is. For as I emphasized above: I do not recommend—nor do I endorse—any brand of dog food. There are so many quality formulas on the market today it would be impossible to judge one of them superior to another without attaining your doctorate and building your own lab.

In every instance today, you must consult the nutritionist of your choice. And that is now possible: You see, Dr. Jack Mara (who you'll meet now) told me yesterday he has six Ph.D. canine nutritionists who just graduated from American universities, and thirteen more in the wings. These people, plus all dog-food companies and veterinary colleges, will now answer any nutrition question you pose regarding your dog, and the material will be correct and noncompany-biased. This is one industry you can trust.

PROTEIN: THE DOG KILLER

Jack Mara, DVM, director of Veterinary Affairs, and head of Hill's Pet Nutrition, Inc. College Program, is sitting at my kitchen table—he's been here six hours—and he's citing one fact after another. He proceeds with the steady beat of a trip hammer, and I sit spellbound with both his knowledge and his lifelong dedication to good dog health care. (He started as a farm-boy-turned-student janitor in Cornell University's veterinary school.)

First Jack rolls a handful of bladder stones out into a bowl. "These stones," he says, "are commonly found in many breeds of dogs." (I've found them in my westies and Lhasas.) "And they cause great distress. They form due to feeding foods with excessive levels of minerals eliminated through the urinary bladder, where they collect and harden. But there's a new diet that will actually dissolve these stones. And for the very first time it's now possible simply by changing the food to avoid what has always been a surgical problem."

Doc's right, but don't forget the dog's water: It, too, can be loaded with minerals.

"One of the elements common to all stones," Jack explains, "is that they form in either acid or alkaline urine, and these foods take advantage of that. The struvite [a composition of magnesium, ammonia, and phosphorus] in the dog is soluble in an acid urine, so we use a diet that produces acid urine to dissolve the stone. Now, magnesium and phosphorus are minerals. But the ammonia is caused by the breakdown of protein, and when the dog has bacterial infection, even more ammonia is produced.

"So the infection must be treated and the protein reduced in the food—and you reduce the ammonia produced.

"By developing a diet that is restricted in minerals and protein and which produces an acid urine, we can sometimes dissolve these stones in as little as two weeks.

"Think how significant this is when male dogs can slough off these stones to enter the penis—to be blocked by the bone that is in there. Can you imagine the discomfort? Well, that usually requires surgery. Plus, the stones can recur. But with the proper diet, the stone is dissolved and does not occur again. These are the types of things we can accomplish through dietary management."

CANNED DOG FOOD

Now let's discuss protein, just you and me. Look at the can or bag of dog food you have in the house. What does it say the minimum protein content is? Let's assume the can says 10 percent crude protein. Well, 75 percent of most canned dog food is water. So that means there's 25 percent dry content.

Okay, divide ten by twenty-five, and what do you get? *You get 40 percent protein.* Folks, day after day, that can be a killing wallop! Incidentally, Dr. Jack Mara tells me that an all-meat canned diet can run as high as 57 percent protein.

Here's what we must look for:

- A good (and actual) protein content for an average growing dog's diet is 25–26 percent.
- For a working dog it's 28–29 percent.
- For an older dog in good health, the figures are 19–20 percent.
- And for a dog with kidney problems, 14–17 percent.

And we've got to consider the nature of the crude protein content. You know, wood chips and shoe leather contain protein.

So now we must consider the biological value of protein, which means how much the dog's body can digest, absorb, and use. Milk, for example, is 100 percent digested, absorbed, and used. Whereas gelatin is 0 percent. Meat products have 75–80 percent value.

DRY FOOD

But let's look at that bag of dry food. Most dry-food protein levels are tested in a range of 15–27 percent. Very rarely will one be listed lower. And the moisture content may vary from 8 to 10 percent (with an average of 9 percent).

The formula for determining the dry weight basis, assuming protein listed (as is) as 27 percent and moisture listed as 10 percent, is:

$$\text{Nutrient dry weight} = \frac{\text{\% nutrient listed (as is)}}{\text{dry matter (100\% water)}}$$

Which figures out to:

% protein dry weight = 27/90 = 30%

So beware of nutrient contents listed on the label. Get your pencil and pad and figure out the actual protein content. It's vital for Pup that you do this.

But notice (when we figure out) that the protein content listed for dry food more closely approximates actual protein content than does canned food's listed figure. Remember this. The canned food (above) went from *10 to 40 percent protein.* But the dry dog food went only from *27 to 30 percent protein.*

The point: You wanted your dog to get only 10 percent protein from that canned dog food—but folks, the poor little guy is actually getting 40 percent.

DISCLAIMER

But know this—please know this—Dr. Jack Mara has always told me that diet alone doesn't prevent or even successfully manage disease. The primary causes, other than nutrition, must also be addressed. "The way you carry on," Jack tells me, "tends to be harsher than I feel is merited."

So know that I am biased. But quite frankly, for the health and long life of your dog, maybe you should be biased, too. So if I wear three raincoats in a storm, I just don't want to get wet. The point being: I love my dogs so much, I want them with me as long as possible.

THE NATIONAL RESEARCH COUNCIL

Jack now emphasizes, "You have to watch what you feed your dog. Some foods are formulated to meet the *minimum* requirements of the National Research Council (NRC), which sets levels for growth and for reproduction. Now many of the foods, because of the ingredients selected, *contain far more than the minimum requirements.*

Matter of fact, it is not an uncommon practice to see a statement that they meet or exceed . . . and people are often impressed that *more is better* so they figure the food in that bag, or can, must be better than the food where the label says the contents merely meet those requirements.

"But excesses of nutrients are very harmful: Consider the bladder stones. Therefore the veterinarian's attention is now directed to foods that contain the optimum or the correct levels of nutrients.

"In no way do I intend to put down the NRC. What I need to emphasize, however, is that the labels (and the foods) relate to minimum requirements, they don't relate to optimum, and they don't discuss maximums. Realize, too, that the Association of Animal Feed Control Officials (AAFCO), a regulatory group of state feed officials, now requires all pet foods to meet these standards.

"What the dog owner must recognize is he doesn't need all that protein, all those minerals, all those calories. And excesses of all these subtly cause burdens to the internal organs of your dogs.

"The real harm," explains Jack, "is these burdens don't show up overnight. You can't tell there's an impending buildup in blood pressure, you can't tell the animal's kidney is slowly deteriorating, because they are born with 65 to 75 percent more functional kidney tissue than they need. So accordingly they have that amount of tissue to lose before they show signs of deficiency, or a defect. And by that time, literally, the horse has left the barn. The result is you must now deal with a diseased kidney."

Remember Muffy: Her diseased kidney was not caused by a poor diet. She was fed the best scientifically prepared food available. Muffy's kidney was destroyed by calcification caused by cancer, and Lhasas are notorious for kidney deficiencies at birth. Still, Muffy was fed too many treats by a loving human partner. We assuredly will talk about this later. But the crux of it is this: It's hard to tell a dog that you love him by denying him, right? How much easier to show him you love him by loading him with a bunch of junk food.

None of us is immune to this. I smile in remembrance of the scene in *Major League*, the spoof-movie about the basement-dwelling Cleveland Indians. Remember? Wild Thing was the pitcher who formerly played for California Penal and threw his last pitch in the movie at 101 miles per hour.

He and two of his teammates were dining in an upscale restaurant that handed patrons a foreign language menu. Wild Thing asked the catcher, an educated sort, if the menu mentioned chili dogs.

I've never known a dog who didn't have a little bit of Wild Thing in him. You won't either. Dogs love treats.

HIDDEN HARM

Back to Jack, who is saying, "All this occurs because the harm is unseen, and because we hype protein and its value, and because people misunderstand the function of protein and assume it is responsible for energy.

"Protein *does* produce energy, but along with carbohydrates, it provides less efficient energy than you expect. Both protein and carbohydrates net about four calories per gram. So if you really want to increase your dog's energy, *add fat to his diet.*"

THE KIDNEYS

"But let's stick with protein and kidneys. Too much protein throughout a dog's life stimulates kidney function, and over a period of time, it causes a loss of that function because of internal pressure upon the filtering system.

"The kidney eventually yields to that buildup of pressure by laying down fibrous tissue," continues Mara. "And when the kidney cell is invaded by that fiber it dies.

"This is because of hyperperfusion. It takes a great deal of pressure for the cell to filter out the material in the urine that has to be eliminated. This filtering process occurs in the glomerulus—the group of cells surrounding the cavity within the kidney, very microscopic in size, through which the blood passes. The blood is retained in the circulation, but the waste materials are eliminated through the action of those cells.

"The more protein the dog eats, the greater the effort required by these cells to eliminate waste materials. And sooner or later, just as a bridge begins to show signs of stress, so, too, does the glomerulus. And its defense is to build up fibrous tissue to give it greater support in a sense, and it therefore replaces the active glomerulus cell with this fibrous tissue. Eventually, it leads to the death of the cell."

You know I'm neither a vet nor a scientist. I'm just a guy who's seldom lived without a dog; the only time spent without one was in college or the service where they were prohibited, and then I kept an eye on them most of the time. Most of us think a dog who drinks a lot of water is healthy, that this is a good thing.

But let me tell you this: If you see your dog beginning to drink large amounts of water, don't smile and be complacent. Your dog may be developing kidney failure. Heed this sign of excess water intake and get your dog to a vet.

OTHER NUTRIENTS

Jack leans back and continues, "I was speaking of protein as destroying kidneys, but other nutrients have the same ability. For example, sodium is in pet foods according to NRC standards in excess of what's needed. You'll find 1 or 1.2 percent of the diet is sodium. But we have plenty of evidence that .04 percent is sufficient. Too much sodium also contributes to retention of fluids within the body tissues, which leads to a greater workload for the heart, which in turn leads to congestive heart failure. Again, that's a largely preventable condition. And excessive levels of phosphorus are also damaging to the kidney.

"Okay," he says, "let's review. Excessive levels of protein can contribute to kidney disease and *26 percent of America's dogs die of kidney failure.*

"Sodium contributes to increased blood pressure and heart disease. Something like *40 percent of all dogs over ten years of age have some degree of heart failure.*

"Magnesium contributes to urinary bladder stones.

"Too much calcium may contribute to bloat, which is a very lethal condition. The mechanism is this: Too much calcium will stimulate the production of gastrin, which is a hormone in the lining of the stomach. This in turn causes what we call a hyperplasia: The stomach-lining cells are increased in size (hypertrophy) and in number (hyperplasia). This occurs particularly in the area of the pylorus, the valve leading from the stomach to the small intestine. This constricts the pylorus and delays the emptying process that contributes, then, to the formation of gas and so forth. This condition can even be found in the stomach of an unborn puppy of a pregnant bitch that is being supplemented with too much calcium."

VITAMINS

I go to the counter and pour Doc a glass of water as I say to him, "Hey, Jack, can a guy walk into a health-food store today, buy some touted dog supplements, and walk out knowing when Pup has consumed all this stuff he's eaten himself to good health?"

Jack smiles and says, "Unfortunately, the answer to that has to be no. When you consider that in both human and animal nutrition, the formulation of diets in determining just the right levels of all minerals, vitamins, proteins, carbohydrates—all of them—is a highly scientific process, requiring computer assistance, and a great deal of education taking years to acquire.

"Then you turn someone loose in a health-food store to impulse-buy or to take the advice of the owner, or a well-meaning friend, and you have just turned a cannon loose in your dog's body. And that's essentially because of this one fact: *The balance of minerals in a dog's diet is so critical that when he has an excess of one mineral, it will influence the absorption of another.*

"For example, too much calcium in the diet blocks the absorption of zinc. And get this: If the dog doesn't have enough zinc, the insulin process doesn't develop naturally, so the dog has an increased tendency to develop diabetes mellitus.

"There is also an increased probability that your dog will develop a skin that is not resistant to disease. Many veterinarians will diagnose a skin problem as a zinc deficiency and be right on, but the real cause is not a lack of zinc in the diet. The real cause is that the dog owner is adding calcium to the dog's food.

"Now, many of the health foods do not contain sufficient amounts of the primary ingredients to do any harm. So they don't do any good, but at the same time, they don't hurt the dog. But they don't stimulate good health, they stimulate the distribution of dollars."

OVERLOAD

"Yet an overload can occur if these additives are stored up in the dog's body. Too much calcium, for example, interferes with the absorption of iodine, which leads to thyroid problems. It also leads to interferences with the absorption of copper, which can end up with copper deficiencies. Copper is an essential nutrient affecting bone formation and bone strength.

"Too much phosphorus in the diet will contribute to blocking calcium absorption. Too much phosphorus also stimulates the parathyroid gland, located in the neck, which is responsible for maintaining normal calcium levels in the body tissue.

"Now the law of the body requires normal levels of all nutrients be maintained in the circulating blood, and the body will do whatever is required to maintain that normal level.

"When nutrients are missing in the diet, the dog's body is then forced to take them from its stores in the tissues, the bone, and the bone marrow, until the body becomes depleted. For example, when the body draws the calcium out of its bones, they become brittle, and the probability of pathological fractures [those not occurring with trauma] goes up.

"When there is too much phosphorus in the dog's diet, the calcium level in the blood plasma drops, and the body calls on the calcium reserves in the bone for replenishment. However, due to the dominant role of phosphorus, the calcium is forced, instead, into the soft tissues of the body and eliminated through the kidneys.

"In women and bitches, this occurs in the breast. In all of us, particularly if we have fatty deposits in our blood vessels—which most of us do—the calcium becomes deposited along coronary arteries or the aorta, narrowing them, and eventually causing a hardening of the arteries. Even worse, the calcium begins to be deposited in the kidney tubules, and once that happens the kidney literally turns to stone."

THE CAUSE OF DEATH

"Some 78 percent of dogs who are autopsied at death have evidence of calcification of the kidney. I can't think of anything more dramatic to say in respect to the penalty of excesses or imbalances in our dogs' diets."

I know it's hard to do—yes, folks, I fail, too! You look down and see those lovely, begging, smashed-in faces with the put-on, suffering eyes, and you reach right for a tidbit. But try not to supplement your dog's standard nutrition with treats. Too many of them are loaded with protein. But once again Jack takes me to task, saying, "We have a good treat, balanced to the dog's life cycle. All you have to watch is calories."

If you must give anything, give nonbasted rawhide knots or strips. But even then you've got two possible problems. The dog chews up the rawhide and ingests the juices or gnawed-off pieces, and rawhide contains a minimum of 70 percent crude protein. Plus, should the dog just flat swallow the strip or knot, then you can easily have intestinal blockage, possibly requiring surgery. Treats, then, can be the killers of dogs. Just as those goodies between meals can be the killers of humans. Don't forget that.

Now we must balance off my antiprotein mania with these realities. Puppies must have protein to grow. Working dogs must have protein to stay in the field. And geriatric dogs also have their unique need for protein. So what does the human partner who wants to keep his dog for fifteen years do? He consults his vet. He consults the new nutritionists. He calls the university vet schools. Then feeds what they recommend.

And as an alternative for those of you who insist on giving your dog between-meal treats: Bake them yourself. There are many recipes. Check any of your dog-supply catalogs. Or read your dog-food labels. Many of them have an 800 number you can call to talk to a nutrition expert.

KIDNEY DIET

Now back to Dr. Jack Mara. He says, "Bill, there's now a diet for kidney disease based on reduction of protein, sodium, and phosphorus, which eases the burden of the diseased kidney. Even kidneys that have been 90 percent destroyed can be kept functioning with this diet adequately to meet the dog's body needs and keep him alive."

AMINO ACIDS

"You see, *most dogs are fed some five times more protein in their daily diet than required.* A protein is valued by its amino-acid contents.

There are twenty-three amino acids required for good health, and they are a part of the dog's body. But the dog's body is able to make, through the food he eats, some thirteen of these amino acids. But there are ten amino acids that we call 'essential,' meaning they must be in the food; the dog cannot make them."

Let me ease in here. I know nothing about chemistry. Doc's the expert. But I do know dog food. I could have served a million meals. I need a sign in the kitchen that says, "Thousands and thousands served."

Anyway, you'll be serving a diet and one day you'll open a can that has a totally different consistency than the previous cans. Usually the difference is that the food from the new can is sticky, it clings to your serving utensil. Or sometimes the food will stink. Or another time the dogs won't eat it, but you can't smell or see anything wrong. Then, too, the food may have shrunk away from the sidewall of the can, or appear with a skim of fat on top, or have the wrong color.

The same goes for dry food. Ask yourself, is it mildewed, greasy, sticky, wet, crumbling, smelly?

I don't care what the inconsistency is, here's what you do: Call the 800 number for that brand of dog food. Most pet-food companies print this number on every can. When a representative answers, she will ask you for the number on the cardboard case or on the can. Give it to her along with your concern or your complaint.

The last time I called I told the company representative, "I'm feeding my dogs their standard diet, but all of a sudden the cans have become soggy; the food sticks to my knife."

She answered, "You're absolutely right. We're having problems with that formula and have yet to find out what's wrong." Then she said the obvious, things like, "We can assure you there is nothing wrong with the product and it will not hurt your dog in any way," and so forth.

Then she added, "We appreciate your calling us and would like to send you two coupons redeemable at your favorite outlet for our products."

And the truth is, she did appreciate the call. The companies must hear from the field to know how their product is holding up. Never hesitate to let them know.

EGG PROTEIN

"The more essential amino acids a protein contains," continues Dr. Mara, " the higher its biological value. Most proteins do not contain all amino acids. The one that does is egg protein: It contains albumen. So there is now a diet based on egg protein. Being composed of the highest quality of most of the essential amino acids, egg has the least amount of waste material. It's all usable. Very little of it is eliminated as waste. Accordingly, a dog with up to 90 percent of his kidney destroyed can still make it on that 10 percent kidney remnant.

VITAMIN MEGADOSES

"Now let's consider megadoses. They are wrong in principle, and they are wrong in fact. First off, megadoses affect the absorption and the metabolic use of other nutrients."

OIL-SOLUBLE VITAMINS

"The oil-soluble vitamins are A, D, E, and K. Being soluble in fat, they are transported through the body by fat and stored in fat. Now, both vitamins A and D are stored in the liver. So even though the doses of A and D you may be giving your dog are below the toxic level, *they are stored and may then rise above the toxic level."*

VITAMINS A AND D

"Vitamin A is responsible for night vision and the health of skin and mucous membranes. It also works with vitamin B and calcium and phosphorus in the orderly maintenance of bone. Very simply, vitamin D causes new bone cells to form, and vitamin A helps take old bone away. There is constant modeling of bone through growth as well as in the adult stage of the dog."

VITAMIN B

"Vitamin B is simply eliminated through the urine hours after it is consumed in excess of the body's requirements. Certain illnesses—or the use of certain drugs—can cause the dog's body to lose vitamin B at an extraordinary rate. Certain medical problems involving the liver, kidney, or heart may require the veterinarian to prescribe increased doses of vitamin B."

VITAMIN C

"Dogs manufacture their own vitamin C; an ability that humans do not have. So there is even less reason to give vitamin C in any manner to a dog."

SUPPLEMENTS

Jack pauses, looks hard at the tabletop, then says, "Bill, there's just no need for supplements to diets, nor for home remedies. There are now foods that take care of most problems a dog can face. Consider the burro, the pack animal that has had an overload placed on its back and is literally caving in as it staggers under that load. And then comes the magic of lifting that load away, and now the burro can live a normal, pain-free life. That's the way it is with our dogs.

"With proper diet [and this excludes table treats] dogs can live free from awful burdens caused by poor nutrition. We take the burden off the diseased heart with a sodium-free diet. We take the burden from the kidney that's being destroyed with excessive levels of protein and sodium and phosphorus. We take the burden of indigestible food from the inflamed bowel. We allow the animal to have bland food that he can digest, that he can absorb. We can provide a consistent diet now to the diabetic dog, so the dose of insulin that's required is stabilized. It then becomes easier for the dog owner to manage diabetes successfully.

"The list goes on. We lift the burden of obesity, the dissolution of bladder stones, food allergies. It is all very exciting now, and very fulfilling.

"But we still have voodoo medicine with us, old wives' tales, fads, miracle claims. To be safe—absolutely safe—the dog owner who just won't feed a balanced diet should give only water-soluble vitamins to his dog, and these are B and C. And these supplements should never contain minerals. And under no circumstances should a dog owner begin giving vitamins A and D to a dog without a veterinarian's prescription.

"Most of all, the dog owner must be ever vigilant in keeping down protein in his dog's diet. That's the killer. That's the kidney destroyer. And I repeat: 78 percent of all dogs autopsied at death show calcification of the kidney resulting from excess protein."

Doc's still talking as we leave the house and I drive him to the Sedona airport laid out on a mesa. He enters the small, twin-engine prop commuter plane. Clouds are building. It's dark to the south, where he's heading, but he's paying no mind. He just keeps talking of dog diets and proper nutrition. I sit through the dark evening awaiting word he made it through. It's something to have that kind of dedication. And you millions of dog lovers should realize that there are literally thousands of men and women, like Doc, who have devoted their lives to the health and happiness of your dogs.

18

Twenty-First-Century Vet Care

In this book we've started a few chapters with humor. But the jokes stop here: Vet care is not a laughing matter.

Three things happened this week important to my life, to you, and to your dog. You may not see them that way in the beginning—but you will at the end.

First off is a letter I received from Dr. Dick Royse.

He writes:

> After years of active practice and a lot of gray hairs, I've been thinking a lot about what is happening to the veterinary profession. This doesn't mean I'm an expert by any measure; only an observer.
>
> In the early years, and until about the past ten to fifteen years, we all pretty well fit the "James Herriot" image. Then a lot of changes began to appear.

MANAGEMENT

First came management. It was the wave of the future; how to treat our clients, increase their numbers, handle employee relationships, and practice income analysis. No problem, we probably needed it.

ADVERTISING

Then the Federal Trade Commission, in its infinite wisdom, determined that veterinarians could and should advertise, so we did—in the yellow pages, mailers, newsletters, and over radio and TV. I'm always amused by a full-page ad in the yellow pages that says, "Dr. John Doe, DVM, spays, neuters, X-rays, does dentistry and medicine." How dumb do we think people are? They know what a veterinarian does. Does Dr. John Doe assume they don't know the difference?

Plus, how can we possibly advertise what we can do that our colleague down the street can't? Or that we can do it better?

MARKETING

Then came marketing. We were told we had to market our services. In so doing, we tried to be all things to all people: retailing pet foods and supplies, grooming, behavioral training, nutrition. There are some good things in there, but it got so mixed up, you couldn't tell if we were a medical facility or a pet flea market. At the same time, we became concerned with public relations so the public would perceive us as the professionals we started out to be. Throw all these things together, and they flat don't fit.

MULTIPLE-CLINIC CORPORATIONS

Now we have corporate practices. I don't mean practices that are incorporated. I mean practices owned by corporations. Some of them, let's say, with thirty clinics in more than one state, with all the managerial controls and interests of a fast-food chain. As a matter of fact, one young corporate vet recently told me, "We're like an ice-cream store. We just have time to scoop a cone and take your change. Everything's based on fast turnover: Don't give us an order that makes us work . . . that takes time. There's no profit in it."

And I thought of the new neuter and spay clinics with their emphasis on vaccinations. They're set up for "poke and go," not for hours of diagnosis and life-and-death surgery.

Doc continued writing:

> We are all familiar with corporate America. Corporations exist and thrive on one single premise—the profit-and-loss sheet. How do we deliver care and compassion to the patient and the client within the rigid policy format of corporate management? Are the patient and the client going to be well served in that effort to produce an acceptable profit-and-loss statement?
>
> Take the multiple-site corporate clinic I recently heard about. A memo came down to the individual veterinarians, saying, "If the customer is not complaining about your bill, you're not charging enough."
>
> **Medical Technology**
>
> Another significant change is the tremendous advances in medical technology that have become available in recent years. The diagnostics and procedures available are endless. So is the cost of delivering these services. It's easy to fall in the trap of using all these things to solve our problems: diagnosis and treatment by the data, if you will.
>
> **The Art of Practice**
>
> We must not discard the *art of practice.* This is a vague term that means different things to different people. To me it means knowing the client, knowing the patient, thinking for them and about them, feeling and observing the case presented you while the ice-cream customers wait.
>
> Also, what if owners can't afford the radiographs, the lab work, the endoscope, the ultrasound, and the complicated diagnostics? Do we refuse service to them? I think not. Offer the best service to the patient that you can. And in so doing you may have to compromise. Which is not necessarily bad medicine. Do what you can given the factors you have to work with. Which, I repeat, is the art of practice.
>
> **Outside Detractors**
>
> Now we have outside factors to deal with such as OSHA, DEA, EPA, humane groups, and animal-rights activists. Is it any wonder that it's

difficult to focus on where veterinary medicine is headed?

We live in a world of change and we must adapt to survive, but remember, every time you change to improve something, you give up something. Let's not give up James Herriot. Let's keep that ideal of individual attention to every patient and client and not end up in a cold and sterile medical environment, lest we end up being viewed as money-grabbers caring only about the P&L sheet. My hope is that we can strike a balance, somehow, that will provide the best for all concerned.

If all this sounds negative, that is not my intent. As I said in the beginning, these are only my observations. And unfortunately, when I review what I've written, I see there are more questions raised than answers given.

I'm approaching the end of my practicing years, so why should I care? I'll answer that. Because veterinary medicine has been my life, and I, for one, care deeply about what happens to the profession I've loved so much.

A LITTLE DOG NAMED MUFFY

The dogs know, but they don't know what they know. The house is filled with it since Muffy lies on her comforter before the sofa as she's dying.

I sit at the kitchen card table and watch her sleep. She is curled into a ball and her head lies on a pillow and now and then, with difficulty, she raises up to see if I'm still there and stares at me with dark and questioning eyes.

It's been so long in coming. I bought her casket in March and now it's late August. A board-certified radiologist had told me she had two weeks to six months to live.

Muffy didn't want to say good-bye. She fought for those six months. But she fought with grace. And in so doing gained the admiration of a large medical staff and my humility at what she had that I could never muster.

It never was our intent to prolong Muffy's life. All we wanted to do was make her comfortable until she told us it was time to go. And we had a way of learning that. Each night I would take her for a ride in the car, and should she find something to bark about—if she was that interested in life—this told me she wanted another day.

I look at her now and remember so many things we shared.

THREE DAYS OF SCREAMING

One Friday afternoon, Muffy started screaming and contorting and pointing to her back with her nose and mouth. I rushed her to our established vet—her pain was so great that she bit the personnel—where she was diagnosed with arthritis. No doubt this was true, but that was not her problem. It soon revealed itself: Muffy was developing a herniated disk.

I asked for pain pills but was refused. Instead, the vet instructed me to administer aspirin. I again demanded pain pills and was given five.

I was later told by an orthopedic surgeon that time is of the essence in surgery for a herniated disk, or the procedure can be useless.

But we didn't know that then. We were told that Muffy was in pain due to arthritis. So valuable time was wasting.

Muffy was in discomfort that Friday night and all day Saturday. Dee continued to call the vet and was continually told to give aspirin. And we kept on hoping Muffy would get better.

But sometime during Saturday, the spine apparently blew, and Dee held Muffy in her arms for hours as the little dog writhed and screamed.

Frantically we tried to summon the vet who had diagnosed arthritis from her X ray. For we couldn't understand what was wrong. We know a little about arthritis: It seldom makes you scream. But the answering service called the vet and got no response, even though it was this vet's turn to be on duty for the community.

The gal tending the answering service told us, "When this happens, and there's an emergency, I try to get a vet in another town. Do you want me to do that?"

Through her efforts, we soon got a call from an out-of-town vet.

The vet could hear Muffy screaming over the telephone. We said we had the pain pills, and the vet instructed us to give her one. We were then told that if she didn't improve we should call and bring her in that Sunday morning.

Muffy's condition grew worse, so Dee called about dawn, and the vet told us to bring her in. I got there fast and the vet diagnosed Muff's plight for what it was and he phoned the big city. The orthopedic surgeon said, "Yes, I will operate on her," and Muffy and I sped away—with her screaming mile after mile after mile.

Five days later, we got Muffy back. She would live, but there would be problems. There had been too much delay in getting her into surgery.

With Dee and me holding the ends of a towel slung under Muffy's belly, we taught her to walk again. And since Muffy had neural damage, she could not control her bladder or her bowels. So another vet taught me how to express her to empty her bladder so she could sleep with Dee at night. And during the four additional years Muffy lived,

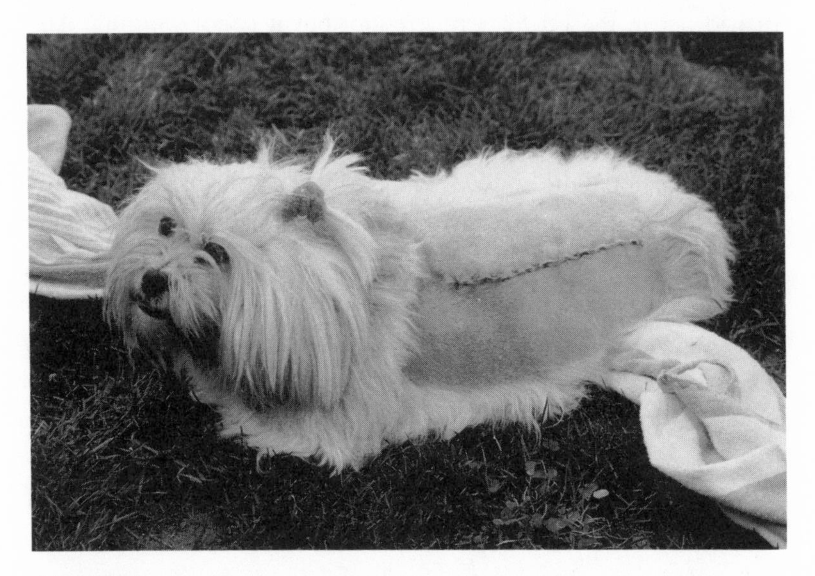

Muffy following her spinal surgery. Note the towel beneath her with which Dee and I helped her walk.

she never could maintain absolute control over her drippings or her droppings. We usually had a wet spot somewhere, a dropping somewhere else.

I've often wondered if the vet on duty for the town, who never answered the phone, or the beeper, ever saw Muffy in some vague way. Ever saw what happened to the life of a little dog. Ever saw what had been done to the lives of two people.

But Muffy was all grit. Though she had minimal neural control, her sense of duty would usually see her make it to the porch before she released. I'll never know how she did it. And she had dignity through it all, and resolve, even though she never lost her sense of shame. You could see it in her eyes. She was so ashamed of the puddles, but she could not help it. So she taught us grace in pain. She taught us self-reliance when crippled.

THAT THING AWAITING ALL OF US

But now it is ending. Yesterday Muffy started with diarrhea and I rushed her to the vet for a power shot but it is not working. And Muffy awakened this morning disoriented, with her left eyelid drooping, her jaw askew. Dee slept downstairs on the floor with her so she could get Muffy to the yard fast. And this morning Muffy and Dee arose before I did and Dee found Muffy with her two front paws on the first step to the staircase. Muffy was trying to climb the stairs to be with me. I will never forget that.

Now Muffy rises to go dump, but she does not know where she is. She walks the wrong direction but somehow self-corrects and finally makes it out the dog door, dragging her back legs over the metal and walking across the concrete (this is the ninety-eighth day in excess of 100 degrees) to reach the sun-dried grass. And why don't I go and carry her out? Because Muffy has told me she wants to do it herself.

She dumps in the yard, but her back legs won't support her and she collapses into the diarrhea and scoots along as I go to pick her up and bathe her and rub her with a towel and lower her back to her comforter.

I wonder again: Could the vet who didn't answer the phone imagine Muffy dragging herself over the metal of that dog door?

And Now Today

I've just called the Las Vegas clinic, and after Dee and I have told Muffy how much we love her, and how much we will miss her, and how much life for us and the dogs will never be the same again—we will put her to sleep. Put her out of her shame, out of her pain, out of her inability to climb the stairs and scootch into the armpit of a sleeping loved one.

But I cannot bury her because we're not in Sedona. So I will take her to a pet cemetery that has a walk-in cooler and she will stay there until I can drive her home.

On the Trail

But having remembered the bad times, I also remember the good, the remarkable. Like that time we all came down the Coronado Trail in eastern Arizona, which has to be the most frightening road in America. There are no guardrails, the road is usually wet, and oncoming cars are driven by natives who delight in speeding and crowding the centerline.

You leave the desert and climb to ponderosas, where in July you'll be flanked by patches of snow. Each mile of the way, the dogs—and Dee—felt my concern. Dee was white-knuckled. Muffy was tense and unsettled. The other dogs, who were very young, caught the doom we transmitted. But somehow Muffy gave the puppies courage. She wouldn't show her terror. And when we stopped beside the road for sandwiches, Muffy ate Dee's and then ate half of mine. We had lost our appetite.

And Muffy was there for eleven Christmases. I remember the time she dragged out the package containing home-baked bones and opened it five days early.

And how Muffy loved to eat. She got potbellied, and I'd joke with Dee about putting a roller skate under her belly. And she hated thunder and would bark at God, telling Him to take it away. And pigeons that once picked out our house for rest irritated Muffy and she'd sit long stretches each day so she could spot them on the skylight and give them canine hell.

I loved watching her standing in the wind, twitching her smashed-in black nose. Smelling what messages nature sent and thinking long and hard of her discoveries. I'd go to her and say, "Tell me," and she'd lift her jaw, straightening her throat, and look at me from the corners of her black eyes and bark and bark. She told me things I'll never know.

A Far, Far Better Place

When I get Muffy to Sedona, she will lie high on the hill beneath the juniper and piñon. Rock squirrels play there and Gamble's quail strut about with that strange oil-can call they love to make. And rabbits will stop and nibble the grass over her resting place. And birds will sing her a song.

Muffy was the most dutiful, the most responsible, and the most valiant living creature I ever met. She's earned her place in heaven. May she romp in the grass fields there with strong back legs and with joy.

A Recounting

So let's recount: Two of the things that affected my life, and yours, and your dogs, were the letter from Dr. Royse and the consequences of Muffy's life and her eventual death. For Royse outlines the vet of the future, and Muffy makes it evident what can happen to your own dog in the hands of a careless and uncaring vet who misdiagnoses and mistreats.

THE PROTEST

Another letter came. It was signed by Ms. Jay Ann Martin of Sonoita, Arizona. She wrote, in part:

> I am writing to you regarding the complaint you filed with the veterinary board.
>
> Last November, I, too, filed a complaint against a veterinarian. Because I believed that the decisions in the cases of many I have observed were extremely biased, I began researching all the Board's decisions that had been rendered during the past four years. Based on that research plus observations of several board meetings, I believe that the Veterinary Board has not decided cases impartially and, furthermore, that the Board has attempted to cover up its biases by falsifying numbers on its mandatory annual reports to the governor. Also I have been in contact with many other complainants who are very dissatisfied about the manner in which the Veterinary Board performs its duties.
>
> We are currently in the process of bringing our concerns to the attention of the governor and the legislature, and we are asking for your help. Because you have been through the experience of having a case deduced by the Veterinary Board, your opinions and comments regarding the Board's performance are the most important criteria to evaluate how well this Board is meeting its obligation of protecting the public and their animals.

There was more, but I had read enough. The Arizona State Veterinary Medical Examining Board had finally met its match. What goes around comes around.

Yes, I lodged a complaint (it is a matter of public record) with this board regarding the vet who diagnosed Muffy with arthritis and would not tend to the emergency phone.

The board discouraged me from appearing and said I would not be able to speak unless the other parties to the complaint were present.

The board threw out my complaint.

I appealed.

The board threw out my appeal.

But now, Ms. Jay Ann Martin has delved into the decisions of this board and makes the following allegations:

The board dismissed 95.6 percent of consumer complaints from 1990 through 1993:

- In 1990, 66 cases were filed and 62 (94%) were dismissed.
- In 1991, 67 cases were filed and 66 (98.5%) were dismissed.
- In 1992, 67 cases were filed and 64 (95.5%) were dismissed.
- In 1993, 73 cases were filed and 69 (94.5%) were dismissed (1 is pending).
- In 1994, 14 cases have been resolved and all were dismissed.

I think it is interesting—and maybe you do, too—that the board found 95.6 percent of all pet owners wrong in protesting the treatment their animal received at the hands of a vet. We must indeed be a very irresponsible and stupid public to be wrong 95.6 percent of the time. Don't you agree? Furthermore, it suggests that 95.6 percent of us don't know a damned thing about our pets.

Ms. Jay Ann Martin has now formed a sizable pet task force to go to the board en masse. She will petition the governor and the legislature for a redress of grievances. She asked me to write a letter to further that aim, so I wrote (in part):

> To whom it may concern:
>
> I find the Arizona State Veterinary Medical Examining Board to be a stonewall agency. Its members form a good-old-boy conspiracy to keep the members of the Arizona veterinary profession intact no matter their brutality, incompetency, or lack of care for both the animal and the client.

No complaint is given objective consideration. The client is judged wrong when he or she submits his or her protest.

The board will not let protesters appear before it or speak (anyway it didn't in my case), and summarily finds for the veterinarian, no matter how damning the evidence is against him or her.

All in all, it is quite clear the board does not exist for any other purpose than to shield its veterinarians from any and all claims and to perpetuate a system of shoddy medical care, public insensitivity, and to maintain a profession beyond accountability.

The Three Events

So that's it: Three occurrences that deeply affected my life and yours, and your dogs. And when I said they would affect you: Do you now see why? For you'll always be needing a vet—and hopefully not—but maybe one day you'll be petitioning your own state board of veterinary examiners for redress. Muffy showed us how this could come to pass.

And Dr. Royse's letter? Well, nowhere have I read a better explanation of the dilemmas facing the veterinary profession today than what Doc wrote.

And Ms. Jay Ann Martin's letter and her work for justice in veterinary care affects all of us. If the public doesn't police its boards, the boards will police the public. If you don't fight for your dog—and in so doing, fight for all dogs—who will? For remember: What you do to my dog, you do to me.

No Good Samaritan

There was a story in this morning's *Las Vegas Review Journal/Sun.* A man and his dog, Baron, were stranded in the desert. They deserted their stuck car with the broken clutch and headed for a highway. Baron did not make the trip well—do you know how hot it is in the desert? Directly in the sun? Probably 150 degrees! And, 85 percent of the sun's rays reflect back up from desert sand. You are broiled on both sides. But suddenly Baron's owner knew both of them were saved. He saw a highway patrol car coming. He waved and shouted and thanked God.

But the patrol car passed him by. It was later reported that the patrolman was after a drunk driver.

However, the patrolman radioed some employees of the U.S. Immigration and Naturalization Service that he was working with on another case. They stopped by. Once again the man knew he was saved: that Baron would not die.

But no. The paper reports that the federal employees would not allow the man to put the dog in their car. The air-conditioning might have saved his life, for at this point the dog could hardly stand.

The man is reported as explaining, "I was bent over my dog, trying to shield him and pour water on him. We were in the sun, right in the sun, and we were pleading, 'Let us get into the air-conditioning. Let us get into the vehicle.' "

Then it is reported that only when Baron started going into convulsions did the workers agree to take them to town.

Then the immigration employees' boss stepped in. He is reported as saying that their service prohibits civilians inside federal vehicles. The workers were under no obligation to help.

"By law they could have said, 'I'm sorry, we can't do it,' " the deportation supervisor is alleged to have said.

Then it is reported that the man said, "The only reason they got in the car is because this guy hounded them, I guess. I don't think they were in dire straits."

He is further quoted as saying, "We are not baby-sitters. We're law enforcement and we have things to do."

The dog's human partner is quoted as explaining, "Every minute I spent pleading with the immigration workers were minutes off my dog's life."

The dog died on the way to the vet.

The supervisor ends the newspaper article by reportedly saying, "Had it been a human rather than a dog [the ride] would have been much faster. We transport prisoners. We are not a taxi."

So you see, friends, too often we encounter man's inhumanity to life. These immigration people are *your* employees; they are paid by you; they are sworn to serve you. Remember what I told the gal at the vet who insisted I stay in the examining room because it was their policy? I told her, "I wasn't there when you voted." Remember that?

Were you there when Congress voted, or immigration service people decided, not to let a dying dog into their air-conditioned car? Were you there when it was handed down as policy to the supervisor, "We are not baby-sitters"?

Well, I have written to the U.S. Immigration and Naturalization Service, 425 I Street, NW, Washington, DC, 20536, and have told them this policy must be changed, plus I have told them the incident is being reported in this book and they will be hearing from America. Did Baron die for nothing? Will other dogs die beside a desert road because the immigration service won't assist them? Write today. (I've given you the address.) For remember: What they do to a dog, they do to you.

Two months have passed, and the immigration service has finally answered my letter. They miss the point of the matter entirely by telling me they've transferred my protest to their California office. California? I asked for redress from Congress, which is in Washington, D.C., not California. Another case of people evading the issue, of ignoring the plight of the dog. Does this mean that people just don't give a damn what dog lovers think?

As this book goes to press, I still have not heard from California. It doesn't matter. California can't do what's supposed to be done: That authority lies with the bureaucrats in Washington I wrote to in the first place.

So will you please follow up my letter—I don't care what year it is—and write?

At the moment, it looks as if Baron died for nothing. And the next Baron will, too.

OUR NAÏVETÉ

We carry our dog into a vet clinic with all the naïveté and trust that we have entering a church to have the dog blessed. It never enters our minds that anything could go wrong. It never enters our minds that the vet may kill the dog instead of healing him.

For we know these doctors have sacrificed to learn. They've taken an oath to be compassionate. But that's not always how it works.

OLD MOSSBACK

By now you know I'm a preservationist and a fundamentalist. You also know that in principle I don't like corporate clinics. I hold to that nostalgic notion of the vet alone in his small domain who knows you on sight, knows the names of all your dogs, knows what your wife's ailing with, and how your kids are doing in school.

This vet has doctored Pup since the day he was born. He knows every shot he's had, every illness, every injury.

He knows what's going to happen to Pup before it ever occurs. And he doesn't need $500,000 worth of equipment to back him up. He practices the art, as Dr. Royse says. His intuitions can be better than an electronic readout.

He is more heart than skill, but his skill is sufficient.

He is more humane than he is scientific.

He is more concerned with Pup's well-being than whether or not he makes enough money to buy a pink Mercedes.

For he exists to practice medicine, not to conduct business.

MBA OR DVM

Why would a person go to a veterinary school to become a doctor and then trade in his stethoscope for a ledger sheet in the pet-care business? Why didn't he go get a degree in business management in the first place? That raises the bigger question: Why would we want to take our dogs to a businessman to have him perform surgery or prescribe medicine?

Well, many of these multiclinic owners employ good vets—vets who at a different time would have opened their own small clinics—as was pointed out this morning when I opened the mail to find a sympathy card with subtly hued cardinals drinking from a fountain fringed with flowers. The card was sent by the corporate clinic where Muffy was put to sleep. It read:

> As your friends, we would like to somehow be able to share the burden of your pain, but grieving is such a personal thing. Still, if there's anything we can do, please let us know. We want to help in any way we can.

That was written by Hallmark, but Hallmark didn't write the rest. It was signed by eleven members of the staff and some wrote more than their names.

So this, too, can be the cold, corporate world of multiclinic vet care?

It makes us all wonder what the hell to do, doesn't it? It makes us all wonder if it really matters whether James Herriot is dead?

THE WELLNESS CLINIC

Know what *wellness* means? I don't. I know the word *goodness.* You use it when you want to say, "Goodness gracious." But wellness is not a word. It is an abomination.

So I walked into a PETsMART that had just installed a veterinary clinic (the vet rents the space), and asked the personable young vet just what the hell *wellness* meant. He didn't know me from Adam, so he told this man-off-the-street, "A wellness clinic is where you get a cursory examination of your pet. We check for apparent disease and we give vaccinations, things like that. This is usually on Saturday. But if you really want a thorough physical examination, I'd recommend you bring your pet in during the week."

Yes, folks, the pet-food-distribution megacorporations are entering the wellness business. So what does this mean to you?

Well, an issue of *dvm*, the news magazine of veterinary medicine, started off with a headline that said: ECONOMY, COMPETITION, CHANGING EXPECTATIONS GIVE FRAMEWORK FOR NEXT ERA IN VETERINARY MEDICINE.

Copy beneath this leviathan banner told us, the local vet's concern is with such corporations as PETsMART that are coming into their areas with large marketing budgets to promote their services.

It is further said that these meagcorporations have tested the market and know where veterinary medicine is headed and this is very intimidating to the local vet. For these conglomerates may direct the future of the profession.

One vet allegedly says, "The income generated by such services as vaccinations, spays, and neuters may have already become a thing of the past for most of us." Remember the ice-cream-cone dispenser? That poke-and-go stuff is what many seek, not any in-depth, time-consuming, thirty-dip confection.

Another vet is reported as commenting, "I agree. I don't think we're playing on a level field when you have venture and investor capital to compete against." This vet further says, according to *dvm:* "These large corporations, at least reportedly, are wanting to use what we have spent years of our lives and thousands of dollars preparing to do as a loss leader so they can sell their ancillary items."

In other words, we'll poke your dog for a few bucks if you'll browse our aisles and fill your cart with rubber toys and treats.

Several pages later, *dvm* then serves up the headline: PETSTUFF TO OFFER WELLNESS CARE; GROWTH PLANNED ON EAST COAST.

Roswell, Georgia——"Petstuff," it is reported, "a publicly traded superstore operation in the eastern United States, has entered the veterinary care arena and plans to open at least 25 wellness-only clinics by the end of the year."

Then an executive of Petstuff is quoted as saying, "The real question isn't do you want change [he's talking to the veterinary profession]—the question is, change is here—do you want to be part of it?"

To me that's like a big-money guy invading baseball and saying, "From now on we play with five bases. Whether or not you want change is irrelevant. It's here. The question is, do you want to be part of it?"

Further down the article it is stated, "Petstuff's plans come in the wake of an announcement by PETsMART, a major competitor, that PETsMART would be shifting the emphasis of veterinary care from wellness to high-quality, high-service."

My wonder is: Where are the James Herriots to go?

Later in this veterinarian magazine, *dvm* calls this invasion of the megacorporations "big-format competition."

So what does all this mean to you?

Let me answer.

The Art of Practice

I was having dinner one night with two vets. One was a board-certified internist. I asked this internal specialist, "If a client brings a dog to you, and explains his history, what is your most favored analytical tool? You know, X ray, ultrasound, blood tests?"

I was floored when the vet said simply, "My hands."

Eleven years of college and the sensitivity of the hands touching that animal tells this vet more than all the sophisticated instruments touted by medical science.

And then I consider the wellness clinic. The people lined up, the vaccinations administered. For, let's face it, folks: This is the era of the discount outlet. The shots are cheaper here. And the vet touches your dog for a minute, and as the PETsMART vet said, "We give a cursory examination. . . . " Is this what you want for Pup?

I sure as hell don't. I want the board-certified internist with those educated hands to spend five minutes, ten minutes, an hour examining Pup. And I will pay for it. For I want to know what's wrong with my dog, and whatever it is—I want it fixed.

THE CHEAPSKATE

Which brings us to a central problem in veterinary medicine. Do you know how many people will not pay for medical care? I know of a westie with bad eyes who was delivered to a vet. The vet told the client it would cost $200 to correct the problem. The client told the vet to put the westie to sleep.

A man had a toy Manchester terrier with a badly broken leg. The vet said it could be fixed for $300. The man left with the tiny dog—to die, or to limp in pain the rest of his life?

That's how much many of us care about our dogs. Did you know that? Would you like to be a vet and agonize over a dog's pain and immobility, only to have a client say, "I can't afford it. Put him down"?

Well, it happens all the time. Another instance of man's inhumanity to life.

So what are we to do?

Megabusiness is invading the veterinary profession to make big bucks.

Multiple-clinic corporations are replacing the individual proprietor practicing at the corner clinic.

So is that all bad? Megabusiness is predicated on lowering your pet-care costs. Does that mean more dogs will get vaccinations? Fewer dogs will now die an agonizing death of diarrhea, and vomiting, and gut-binds, and impaired locomotion? Or does it mean hit-or-miss medical care. "Cursory examinations," as they are called.

And what of the multiple-clinic corporation? There are faults. For one thing, they assume all vets are interchangeable parts. You'll have an appointment with a vet you really like, who has proven his or her ability to care for your dog, and by the time you get to the clinic, you're told that this vet has been transferred to another corporate-owned clinic on the other side of town. You're told, "Dr. So-and-so will see you." I don't want Dr. So-and-so. My dog and I feel comfortable with the other vet.

And yet, just such a clinic can give you the best medical care your dog can receive. With one notable exception. If your dog is ever really sick, terminally sick, and you will not let him die—then head for one of the state university veterinary medical schools. That's where the state of the art is practiced. That's where the best minds are. That's where the exotic equipment is. That's where your dog can be saved, if he can be saved at all.

AN ACT OF KINDNESS

And what of the corner vet? One time a police dog was struck by a speeding car and left to die in the road. But a compassionate young lady ran to him, dragged him to the curb. She wanted to save the dog, to care for him, to keep him. But each vet who examined the dog told her there was no way the dog could ever walk again. (Know this: There are vets who do not like for you to make them work. Their job is easier just giving shots.)

The police dog's foot was crushed: best it be amputated. Best yet, the dog be put to sleep.

Well, this lady was engaged to a young attorney who knew Dr. Royse. So he brought his fiancée and the dog to Doc and Doc looked at the broken leg, the crushed foot, and said, "I'll do what I can."

The dog stayed in Doc's clinic two months. And then he got up and walked out. The young attorney asked Doc, "I know it will be a lot of money but what do I owe you? I'll find some way to pay you."

And Doc told him, "It would be so much, there'd be no way to figure it . . . there is no charge."

What corporate clinic would give such latitude to one of its vets? Matter of fact, corporate clinics have quotas. Each vet's daily receipts are tallied; then for the week, for the month, the year. And those who lag are exhorted to find more charges.

And then you turn right around. Some agency may pay a few bucks to put down injured strays. But the vet is too compassionate. So the dog is doctored and saved and adopted out—through the back door.

There is no end to the stories I've gathered over—what is it?—sixty years. Or did I start inquiring that young? It's been a long time.

And what of the tests? Are they always needed? A vet can usually spot parvo for what it is. But the clinic may well have a policy that tests must be made. So there are tests and there are charges. Tests and charges to learn what the "practice of the art" would have told the corner vet in the first place.

NOT WITHOUT FAULT

But the corner vet is not without fault. Consider the English setter the vet had doctored all his life for arthritis of the back. But the doctor had to leave town, so he turned the case over to a referred doctor. You could look at the setter and know what was wrong with it. But the client took the dog to the fill-in vet, and that vet charged $270 for tests to determine what was wrong with the dog.

THE VETERINARY PROFESSION

Good vet, bad vet. It goes on and on and on. But know this. No matter the format in which the veterinarian works, 99.9999 percent of them are St. Francis of Assisi. It's the institution that may be wrong, not the vet. The clinic's way of doing business may be wrong, not the way the veterinarian doctors your dog.

Corporate clinic, sole proprietorship, megabuck operation. What's best for your dog, for your budget?

These are decisions you must make. And who is to help you do it? In the end it all boils down to your best gut-hunch. Be like your dog: FIDO. Remember his miraculous scent, sight, hearing, touch, taste, and empathy. Be like him. Use your own feelings. What does your sixth sense say about the clinic you just walked into? The vet you meet? The way he or she looks at and handles your dog? How they handle you?

Join a dog club; ask the members who they use for a vet. Ask your neighbors if they've heard any horror stories about the vet down the block. Or ask your co-workers about their vet, no matter where he or she practices.

In the last analysis, read your dog. He'll tell you immediately what he thinks of the guy or gal when you enter the examining room. If Pup's leery, you be leery, too. If Pup (though in a state of suppression because he's in a clinic, as Doc Royse told us) leaps up and wags his tail and licks the guy or gal, you may have found the doctor of Pup's choice.

I know it's all real iffy. But we all go through it.

And Just to Make Sure

So don't be naive, don't assume the best. Be critical. Be careful.

If the vet wants to give a shot, ask what it's for.

Ask about the side effects.

Ask how much it costs.

Ask how many will be needed.

Ask if there is any alternative.

Ask, ask, ask.

And that's what this whole chapter is about. *To prepare you to be a better pet owner by becoming a better vet scrutinizer.*

19

Life Can Be Good

They say you can't fight city hall. But should enough people bang on the door, it'll finally open and you will be heard. Where we, ourselves, endure the deficiencies of government, when it comes to our pets we refuse to have them suffer anymore.

Realizing we have now entered that age where we serve government—not the other way around—I was vaulted up, I became jubilant, I was near delirium when *finally* the Arizona Pet Task Force brought the Arizona Veterinary Medical Examining Board before a joint legislative committee.

The Day of Reckoning

This book was finished two months ago. But I waited. I hoped. I kept remembering Muffy. And then miraculously it came to pass—quick, fitting, and final. The Vet Board was summoned to answer the people at an Arizona State Legislative Interim Meeting.

The co-chairman of this event, Representative Lori Daniels, explained this was a *sunset review*, which means: The joint committee of senators and representatives would decide whether or not the veterinary board continued, or if it was to be *sunset.*

This Lori Daniels was a force: She talked distinctly but impassionedly. She was there to conduct business. She had over one hundred people gathered to fight the board, and she let everyone know the committee was going to get to the facts . . . and that was it. Any display, and you're out of here, was her unstated ultimatum.

There were so many protesters in attendance, they filled the hearing room and flowed both directions down the outside hall.

The television crews were so many, and so closely set up, that the audience had a hard time seeing the panel.

There were so many charges lodged by the protesters that the meeting ran over and the co-chairman couldn't get to her quorum meeting.

All because of a dog, a cat, a horse.

It was so beautiful. So correct. So just. So called for. When a board so usurps its authority as to be repugnant to the people it is supposed to serve, and exists essentially to protect its own kind, no matter the charges brought against its profession—to see it knocked down! To see that vet board collectively gasp and struggle and finally realize—it's all over. What a day!

Let me tell you about it.

The Reckoning

You remember Ms. Jay Ann Martin of Sonoita, Arizona. The gal who polled the many people whose pets had been misdiagnosed, or mistreated, or in some other way mishandled—even to their deaths—by veterinarians? And you'll recall when those people appealed to the vet board in defense of their "kids" they were ignored, their petition thrown out.

Remember?

The State Capitol

The sun shone so brightly that morning. I stood before the capitol building but a moment, then turned northeast to enter the House of Representatives. I was alone: an hour early, for I had flown in on the red-eye from Nevada.

I sat in the coolness of the hearing room with the eggshell walls, tan carpet, and blue chairs. It was mausoleum silent. Mincing staff members came and went. One angling name plaque to the left, another to the right, the third just straightening them parallel to the bench's modesty panel.

Then the protesters entered. Silently, hopefully, questioningly: for they knew not how it would go. They had fought this board so many times to no avail and had been rebuffed and laughed at and, in a collective smirk of the vet board, kicked out.

To hope—

The Hearing

The petitioners came tentatively to the microphone. They were mostly women, unaccustomed to speaking, frightened to appear before so many people. Their voices were soft, and the PA system was never turned up, so my taping of the proceedings was fuzzy and garbled. Some of the women cried. But all of them braced, and eventually leveled their subdued voices, and they created a tumult.

We all know this, but so many vets in America have yet to acknowledge this truth. Don't ever, ever, ever get a woman mad at you. The only thing worse is to make a woman mad at you over the mistreatment of her children. And, folks, that's where the veterinary medical board made its biggest mistake.

Had these protesters sought out a vet to heal or help a dog or cat or horse? No. These protesters had asked that vet to help their "children," "a member of the family," "their kid." And something went wrong and the "family member" either suffered or died. Then when these protesters went to the vet board to have something done about it—so other pets would never suffer the same consequence—they were rebuffed.

Well, never turn away a woman seeking justice for her kid. Never, never, never.

Though meek in voice and tightly controlled in demonstration, these women, nevertheless, charged the vet board with crimes called out in the Bible, in common law, in standard veterinary practice, and in fair expectations of humaneness and competence for any person touching an animal.

The atrocities were submitted with the cadence of a trip hammer. Some came in writing, such as:

> For an hour this vet beat my horse with a board trying to load him into a trailer. The horse died. When I complained before the veterinary board, I was told the veterinarian's actions were within the accepted practices of the veterinary community.

But the majority were oral, and they went on and on.

"I took my ten-pound dog in to have her spayed," said one lady, "and she came back with her jaw broken in two places . . . spitting teeth."

"I was a vet tech and I turned in the vet I worked for. . . . I saw him do things so I charged him with illegally dumping animals in the dump, beating a cocker spaniel until there was blood . . . and I had other witnesses see this. But the board ignored my complaint."

"My horse left the hospital with total body infection and when I called the vet board to get a complaint form I was asked by a member of the staff, 'Why are you doing this to poor Dr. . . . ?' "

"We have seen botched surgery, overdose on anesthetics, general mismanagement, and it is all stonewalled by the board."

"There have been falsified records, pain with no pain killer, and yet, when telling the board this, I never received a response."

"I held my cat as he was being put to sleep and the vet missed the vein three times in forty minutes. Know what that's like to hold the friend you love . . . waiting for him to die . . . for forty minutes? Then the tech did the job in three seconds."

THE VELVET HAMMER

Since everyone had to register to speak in order, it finally came Ms. Jay Ann Martin's time to appear. I had never seen her before. She was a slight woman, not presumptuous, very low-keyed in her testimony. She told the committee many things, including:

> The board is nothing more than a rubber stamp saying nothing has gone wrong. The board tries to justify its hiding this away by stating complainants are either liars, or so misguided by their emotional complaints that the board is unable to tell if the vet in question was negligent.
>
> However, numerous complaints have been initiated not by emotional pet owners, but by veterinarians, and all these complaints have also been dismissed. Even a vet who is a former chairman of the board complained that the current board did not investigate his case thoroughly and made inaccurate statements in rendering its decision.
>
> In another case, a vet lodged a complaint against a member of the board. Of course the complaint was dismissed. But then the board initiated a complaint of its own against the complaining veterinarian.
>
> Attorneys who have dealt with the board have also been highly critical of the board's bias and unprofessional behavior.
>
> Tapes of the proceedings have supposedly been misplaced, or are unintelligible, or erased. Not only has this board concealed information from the public, but it has apparently made false statements to legislators when they tried to obtain information.

When Ms. Jay Ann Martin sat down, another protester told the committee:

> A vet operated without sterile instruments, practiced medicine under the influence of drugs, failed to examine animals before surgery, kept inadequate patient records, and provided vet care services without a premises license. The board eventually threw out the

> charges, saying the vet board could not find any violation because the board felt the drug problem contributed to the animal abuse.
>
> Also, at the time of my complaint, there were five other cases against this vet, all of them concluded with no violation. I finally decided the board simply did not care. I recently learned this vet was found guilty of no violation for all charges filed against him.

And it kept going. The charges were: "They're protecting their own keisters."

"A total display of incompetence."

"We need a board that takes responsibility for the care of our pets."

"The board will not find against a colleague no matter the violation."

"Their motto is 'Thou shall not speak out.' "

"The board's protecting their derelict fence."

"Our review of the past several hundred cases before the vet board shows the board votes as a bloc."

And then there was the pivotal committee-provoking statement made by a slight lady who raised on her toes to reach the microphone. She told the committee, "Even here today there are three members of the vet board sitting in front of me in this hearing room, and they've found these proceedings very hilarious."

Don't you think those legislators' heads snapped up and their faces turned stony? Suddenly things really changed.

The Attorney

I don't know who hired him, or whether he came as a "friend of the court." The next witness was an attorney—but not an ordinary attorney. He was blind. And do you know what a blind attorney brings to court with him? A seeing-eye dog. Isn't that beautiful? The protesters now have a defender standing there with his fingers on the podium deciphering braille, and his blind brown eyes staring straight at the unseen committee, and his ten-year-old yellow Lab named

Bill Gibney, with Legal beneath his feet, tells the committee how his hundred clients feel about the veterinary board.

Legal sleeping behind him on the floor. Could Hollywood casting have topped this?

Then in a quiet but telling way, Bill Gibney, attorney-at-law, with dog at side, began speaking.

His voice was soft. He did not display emotion. He was like an accountant reading a ledger. But if you listened closely, off in the distance, you could hear the sound of mortars. Gibney didn't have to throw them. His soft words were made of dynamite.

"I represent one hundred pet owners," he said.

"I have had extensive contact with government," he underscored for the committee, "and I have never seen a board as inept and inefficient as this board. . . . This board should be dissolved."

Then the charges came:

"We do not need a bad, incompetent board.

"We're tired of politics, and rhetoric, and lack of action. We want to be heard.

"We want these things stopped. Cruelty, malpractice, drug abuse, unlicensed and uncertified techs administering anesthetics. Or techs performing neutering. And the denial of public records by the board. The falsifying of public records."

Gibney did not flounder as his finger coursed those bumps on that thick sheet of beige paper.

He kept charging.

"I, too, had a case before the vet board regarding my mother's dog," he said. "They summarily dismissed my case. But get this—the minutes of my hearing have been falsified.

"The board says the protesters are too emotional about the loss of their pet. Does that mean the complaint is without merit? If I lost a member of my family, do you not think I would be emotional? Do you not think you would be emotional?

"The general purpose of this board is to protect the public: *but they support bad vets, they hurt good vets, and they have a general disregard for the consumer. . . .* "

THE BUZZWORD

Again the combined legislative committee's heads snapped up when Bill Gibney said "consumer." This is one of today's alert words in government. *Consumer!*

The consumer is nearly sacred now. Do not cheat. Do not hurt. Do not ignore the consumer. Why, we even have departments protecting consumers. We have regulations and statutes and ordinances for consumers. *And, it is said, legislators believe that consumers vote.*

Bill Gibney was smart. He did not identify the protesters as pet owners. Possibly you can ignore a pet owner in America, but never a consumer. Not now.

Then Gibney began dissecting the board. "Why [is there] a majority of vets on the board?" he asked. "Why?" (This is a seven-man board composed of five vets and two laymen: one for livestock, the other for pets.)

Gibney charged, "They vote as a bloc. You think those two laymen serving on the board can make any difference? Two voices against five are very silent. Two voices against five can never constitute a majority.

"Why should we have a majority of professionals on this board who are investigating the very people they are protecting?

"And the way they do business—you go before them and they throw you out." (Remember, they threw Muffy and me out.) "Guess who you appeal to?" asked Gibney.

He answered, "You appeal to the same damned board." (Remember Muffy and I appealed to that board?) Gibney continued, "You appeal it to a board and they're the ones who grant or deny your right to appeal. That's their second shot at it. And if they do for some reason grant your appeal, they hear it a third time.

"What are the chances of ever winning when you go back to the same board three times?"

(Remember, they threw Muffy and me out the third time?)

STANDARDS OF PRACTICE

Then one of the senators asked Gibney, "Then why don't these people take the vet to civil court?"

And Gibney answered, "It is so hard to prove anything in court because there is no standard of care in the vet industry. The standard of care is based on finances: Can you afford the procedure or not?"

TIME-OUT

This is an interesting charge Gibney makes. So let's call The Wizard of Wichita, Dr. Dick Royse, and check it out. I ask Doc, "Is it right that there is no standard of practice for veterinary care in America?"

Royse answers, "It's the truth. We just rewrote the practice act in the state of Kansas. And this point was addressed. It is a very difficult area to establish rigid standards of practice because it is such an individual thing.

"For example, one vet may say the dog needs a cast, the next one says, 'No, I think he needs a pin,' and the next one says, 'Hardly. What this dog needs are bone screws.'

"So you get into medical opinions, which, you well know, Bill, are arguable.

"So what they did here in Kansas is set forth a state inspection service whereby facilities will be inspected. And there are some pretty rigid requirements for everything from facilities to provide emergency care, to sanitation, to qualifying people, et cetera.

"Thus, people would at least have redress if the vet were not conforming to the very basics. *For you know, the old standard of practice has always been whatever was usual in your area."*

God, I love Royse. He always makes such clear and simple sense.

Then he concludes, "In other words, the question is answered, 'Is this the manner in which the next ten veterinarians in your area would have handled this case?' "

Having answered our question, we turn back to Gibney standing before that legislative committee.

A Just Wind's Blowing

Gibney's telling the committee, "Things around the country are changing. We're finding that to have experts on boards leads to complacency. Leads to unfair results.

"Plus we need to make a change in reporting. You know we don't really care about administrative infractions. It's violations in tending pets that demands our scrutiny. We want violations spelled out in a separate report so the legislature can tell if the board is doing its job.

"And henceforth, make it possible for a person to call the board and find out if a vet has had any complaints against him.

"Then finally," demands Gibney, "either sunset this board—do away with it—or remove the members of this board, or have them resign of their own accord. It will be said we need a board to license vets. That can be done without a board. We just don't need an incompetent board protecting incompetent vets."

The Legislative Committee Acts

That was it. Testimony finished.

Madam Chairman was swift. A motion was tendered from the bench by Representative Rubin Ortega, "I move we reduce the life of this board from ten years to two." The purpose would be to have the board accountable to a sunset review every two years; to make the board more readily accountable.

The notion passed unanimously.

Then Madam Chairman revealed, "The Auditor General will be asked to audit this board at its first opportunity."

Gibney later told me, "That audit will dissect every case that came before the vet board. That audit will tear this board apart."

Then Madam Chairman noted, "Before the next legislative meeting, this committee will make its recommendations for new procedures regarding this board. We are adjourned."

The Book Is Finished

Everyone filed out of the cool, eggshell-toned hearing room. But I was from out of town. My plane wouldn't leave for hours. So I sat. Sat and realized that at last Muffy was heard. Matter of fact, all the Muffys were heard.

Later I moseyed from the House of Representatives and sauntered into the midday sun. An Arizona sun is so startling. And I turned north, facing up toward Sedona a hundred miles away. And said in a soft voice, "Sleep well, Muffy. You—and all the sweet creatures in fur coats—won this morning. Now some other Muffy won't have to drag her back legs in her leavings, or suffer the scorching-hot metal frame of the dog door as she pulls her useless legs across it."

Again the old sadness flushes over me. I take a deep breath and shake it off as I say beneath my breath, "Run in God's green fields, Muffy. Run, Muffy, run."

The taxi comes, and I sit in its rumpled, split-vinyled seat and displace myself from the homicidal traffic. I realize what happened here today is a wake-up call to every board of examiners in the United States. Plus, it's also a wake-up call to the American Veterinary Medical Association (AVMA), which provides 80 percent of the malpractice insurance that veterinarians buy.

In a recent malpractice bulletin from the AVMA, there was a little blurb explaining that the standard-of-practice tradition is not holding up. It is now being attacked in the courts. I don't know what the future holds, my fellow dog lovers, but I'll bet you a bag of kibbles that there are going to be changes coming all over this nation.

I pay the cabbie and step out before the Phoenix air terminal. There is a roaring of jets, the cacophony of horns, the cry of redcaps, the mumbled anguish of travelers. But I do not hear them as I tune my ear just right. For I hear the soft wind blow in the piñons above Muffy's grave. I hear the Gamble's quail call, and see the rabbits scurry, and realize: "Life can be good. You hear that, Muffy," I must say. "Life can be good."

In memorial: Muffy